RIVER OF DECEIT

Gabriel Zeldis

Order this book online at www.trafford.com
or email orders@trafford.com

Most Trafford titles are also available at major online book retailers.

Printed in the United States of America.

ISBN: 978-1-4269-9400-5 (sc)
ISBN: 978-1-4269-9401-2 (e)

Library of Congress Control Number: 2011915970

Trafford rev. 09/02/2011

 www.trafford.com

North America & international
toll-free: 1 888 232 4444 (USA & Canada)
phone: 250 383 6864 ♦ fax: 812 355 4082

Gabriel Zeldis
26 Perry Street
Dover, N.J. 07800
973 361-8456
Lucidity@hotmail.com

To Whom IT May Concern,

I want to be an answer to prayer. Singer, front-man looking to get into a band and gig. Hard worker, I don't do drugs or alcohol. Looking to make it.

Yours Truly,
Gabriel Zeldis

Gabriel Zeldis
26 Perry Street
Dover, N.J. 07800
Lucidity@hotmail.com

To Whom It May Concern,

I would like to put my book in stores. I have four published books. If this is your line of work please email me at your earliest convenience. Thank you for your time.

Sincerely,
Gabriel Zeldis

Gabriel Zeldis
26 Perry Street
Dover, N.J. 07800
973 361-8456
Lucidity@hotmail.com

To Whom It May Concern,

I would like to sell my book in stores. I have four books written and published. I was seeking an opportunity such as this. Please feel free to contact me at your earliest convenience. Thank you for your time.

Sincerely,
Gabriel Zeldis

Gabriel Zeldis
26 Perry Street
Dover, N.J. 07800
973 361-8456
Lucidity@hotmail.com

Dear Madam,

I have been trying to get picked up by publishers, although I'm trying some other companies that might deal with other merchandise other than just books. I tried some car companies to see if they sponsor new writers. When I started hearing back from the companies in the book industry I surprised to see how many places are charging money. I have spoken to many self publishers. I hope everything is going well.

Sincerely,
Gabriel Zeldis

Songs of the Black Angels

The world became at peace…
Violets are carried by the river.
Those that I love are close to me.
Colorado is the forgotten dream.
Someday I'll make it and live
Where I want to live.
The dawn is newborn.
I once had a dream when
I was a child running in Switzerland.
And that was to live in peace.
I remember the mountains.
I was five years old.
Now I live in America.
And I'm striving for the dream.
I'm watching my dreams before my eyes.
I consider the future.

Songs of the Black Angels

Someday I will live in the mountains.
Being a Swiss citizen I dream of this.
But as my dreams fade I look around.
I remember when I dated Katie Mccoy.
I met her at Obsidian University.
She was sitting outside of the classrooms
Waiting for me.
We went to Resica Falls together.
" So do you go out to clubs?" She asked me.
" No I live too far away. Pennsylvania
is too far from the city to go out."
The beautiful moon was in the sky.
And the noon sun shone.
" She asked, " What kind of music
Are you into?"
" I'm into trance," I said.
" I like house and tribal," she said.
" I also like tribal funk," I said.

Songs of the Black Angels

Katie looked at me in the eyes.
" What are you doing Josiah Young?"
" I like the mountains," I said.
" I don't know what I'm doing this for," I said.
Katie was a raver.
She had short blonde hair and was cute.
She had piercings.
What I realized that day with Katie
Was that things needed to work out.
The Beatles played on my car stereo.
The future was before me.
The beautiful future.
Peoples' lives are precious.
But there are dragons,
There are things in the world that cause pain.
My heart needed to heal and once my heart
Did my life would.
The future had everything to do with things.
For the future was in the making.
Through Jesus' forgiveness Josiah Young
Became Eagle Hawk and Whitney became
Super Falcon. Others in the world became
Super heroes including the black angels.

Songs of the Black Angels

They called the world New Zion.
The Cure would go onto tour.
I Josiah Young am Eagle Hawk.
I am a courageous super hero
That plays in the bands Crying Buddha and Ministry.
Crying Buddha is known as The Cure.
The Cure is a ten piece band composed
Of nine black angels and I Josiah Young.
Black Angels have black wings
Instead of white wings, though their still angels,
Just stronger.
The Cure plays music while others
Crime fight. The music is used
For spiritual warfare and has been
Known to confound governments.
We spent the afternoon by the river,
Watching the waterfalls.
Katie was a sensitive girl, a warm soul.
And I felt in that time that our souls were
Led together. We spent the afternoon
Together and she dropped me off
At Obisidian University. That was the last
I saw her.

Songs of the Black Angels

The buses ran outside the amphitheater,
Red Rocks, April 22nd 2012. We were
Known super heroes. I as Eagle Hawk
Chose to protect civilization. I chose to
Protect and serve. I played a Stratocaster,
And I worked as Josiah Young when I
Was with the band. The Black Angels
And I were known as The Cure.
The prophetic sounds of The Cure
Played through the speakers. Josiah Young
Sang to the crowds.
I was working early that spring, not
Long since winter. When I met Rachael.
Rachael was a Super Hero too. She was Ice. Rachael
And I seemed to get along very well. I
Remember the stones in my
Rings turned red like fire when I met her.

Songs of the Black Angels

" Eagle Hawk nice to meet you I'm Rachael
Your soul mate." The white and grey statues
Were all around and there was a stone statue
Of David as an angel. He held a sword.
There was a sun in the sky. A sun
In another universe. The sun was red.
" So what do you say we get into
Something a little more comfortable."
I like what I was feeling for Rachael.
And never before did I think that I would
Only be happy with this person. Rachael
Had been dating another person when I
Met her. After we met my life changed.
I was infatuated with Rachael, I
Had a huge crush on her. She was
Very into me. The red sun shone brightly.
" Eagle Hawk ride with Falcon,"
Lucern said. We'll take the van.
There were dragons in front, large
Dragons. We got into the vehicles
And drove towards the dragons.

Songs of the Black Angels

Dragon fighting was a way of life,
Invented by people. We drove up to
Volcanoes and got out of the vehicles.
The dragons were flying out of the volcano.
" Quick take the Rocket Launchers. The super heroes
Began firing on the dragons. Dragons
Were falling dead. I watched my life
Flash before me as I fired. I remembered
Wrestling and I remember doing drugs. I
Remembered laughing when I was in Colorado.
The rockets were launching and launching.
Falcon picked up a machine gun and
Began blowing off rounds.
I had waited my whole life
To be Eagle Hawk and to belong to
The superheroes. Maybe it was because
The world was at peace, maybe it
Was the wars but my life flashed
Before me. And I heard others calling.

Songs of the Black Angels

Dragons were falling from the sky
As we unloaded ammo at them.
When I was a child I thought of peace,
I dreamed that was how I would live my life.
Somewhere maybe in the hills of Colorado.
Lucern, Claw, Hood and Blue Falcon were backing
Super Falcon and I as my conscience started
Crying within me. Dragons were falling
And then I looked into a dragons eyes
And I saw it, evil. The very thing that ravaged my peace. Day
After day. Night after night.
Before I had met Rachael I was
Single I dated some but meeting
Rachael changed my life. I unloaded
Rockets from the weapons.
I started thinking of Rachael and
How much I loved her. I thought
About us laughing and I could hear
Her saying, " I love you."

Songs of the Black Angels

Nothing compared to my love for Rachael.
I loved her so much, that was life
In Colorado for me, love. I thought
About Rachael every day. I couldn't get
Her out of my mind. That's all I
Wanted to think about was Rachael. She
Was the girl of my dreams. We fired off rounds.
I loved Rachael, I loved her so much.
Maybe it was loving some one that
Brought me so close to things. It
Must have been that the world was
At peace. But my life was far from ok.
The dragons pillaged me and pillaged
Me in my sleep. Rachael said I was
'A real man.' I had a goal and
That was to take down all the dragons
That I could so that I could have
A life of my own. A life for me
And a life for Rachael.
After we used our ammo we
Took off. " Todd this is Eagle Hawk
You have some dragons to clean up."

Songs of the Black Angels

I bought the cathedral in front
Of our property and it saved me. My place
Was still the bachelor's pad, but
Buying the cathedral gave me more space. I
Put a rock on Rachael's hand and I
Took things slow. Rachael had been
Raised by nuns. The David statue was
My love for Rachael. I pulled past it
Every time I took the car to drive .
Rachael wanted to meet a guy
That made a lot of money. She met me
A wealthy singer and a super hero.
As a person Rachael was a secretary,
And she knew the meaning of hard work.
The David angel stood with a sword and
A statue of what appeared to
Be Helen of Troy was close by.
The stone caught the sun
And the David angel was illuminated.
There were angels carved in the stone,
Far away from heaven David's sword
Caught the light and the light brought
The statues to life.
God is a creator,
Therefore, God is for life
And that is for us to be alive.
But every time I drove I
Passed that David that was an angel.
It was my love for Rachael.
Otherwise I wouldn't know what it was
I loved her so much.
My affiliation with crying Buddha
Made my career skyrocket.
I was one of the
Best singers in the world.
I hadn't married Rachael
I just gave her an engagement ring.
But my love for her was profound.

Songs of the Black Angels

The Black Angels sang about loving God
And as time passed Rachael and I grew tight.
Eventually we married.
I would never forget the statue of David as an angel.
This was a Gothic paradise.
People wore black and went to concerts.
When they weren't at a concerts they were at clubs.
The Cure played the club circuit.
We played a lot of dance music.
Dance as a form of expression,
And people danced to trance music.
Like Indians all through the night.
This story is about
Rachael and me and my love for her.
It's difficult to put to words
How I felt reaching out and
Touching my closest friend.
Or what she meant to me.
She meant the world to me.

Songs of the Black Angels

When I looked into her eyes I
Would feel as though I was in heaven.
I felt safe and close to God.
She knew she meant the world to me.
The statues were grey and black in the
Light and when it would rain
The statues would look like real life.
Rachael was my soul mate and a big fan.
I just don't know,
Loving someone as much as I loved her was probably only
Meant for heaven.
We weren't in heaven but
It was like we were.
We weren't and so life wasn't easy.
Rachael had long, black hair
And blue eyes like a baby.
She was a very good artist.

Songs of the Black Angels

So my relationship with Rachael
Is in the angels' music.
The black angels would often
Sing of our love because it was
Glorious and humane.
I can't think of many humane
Things in this world.
We loved one another
And walked towards the golden sun.
When we held we didn't want to let go.
I just wanted to say what she meant to me.
She meant the world.
We lived in a large mansion
In upstate New York.
We had two pictures of me when I was a baby
With our pictures.
When she thought of me she cried.

Songs of the Black Angels

As two we dwelt under heaven.
And two worlds collided.
I was in love with her,
And I never wanted it to end.
Our jobs got in the way.
What I loved about Rachael
Most of all is that she was a Super Hero.
We were known Super Heroes.
But people didn't know our identities.
There was only one Messiah and
That was Jesus Christ.
My relationship with Rachael was beautiful.
We shared so many moments.
" So Josiah what are we
Doing today? Are we going to spend
The day together? Yes, yes. We are going
To spend all day together as long as you want to."
" I do," she said. " I do."

Songs of the Black Angels

Rachael's last name was Diowa.
We danced to the music on that morning
Everything was perfect and beautiful.
All the stars came into focus.
I am a star.
A star from another universe.
Stars are intricate creations.
Stars are like angels in the world.
As a star I'm a unique creation.
Rachael married a star.
And I gave to her only the best.
We didn't have children
And our relationship was pure love.
It was all alright. The world was a cold
Place and ridden with crime.
As super heroes we were in
The crime fighting business.
Rachael Diowa.
Josiah Young, and Rachael Young forever.

Songs of the Black Angels

Rachael and I live on through
Music from angels.
We lived in a mansion and faced the world.
The architecture was from a time.
"What are we to do tomorrow?"
" It's Sunday we get the whole day together."
" We do, what are you drinking?"
" Merlot all day," she laughed.
" Then it's Merlot for me too," I said.
" Rachael I love you and I
Want to spend my life with you.
Nothing will ever get in the
Way of my love for you." I said.
" I love you too," she said.
" Well maybe we can go hiking
In the mountains," I said.
" The Adirondack Mountains…"
" Well when are your studio sessions
Scheduled for?" She asked.
" Monday through Friday, I left
The weekend open for us," I said.

Songs of the Black Angels

" Oh, you didn't have to do that. I wanted
To go and check things out." She said.
" Well the studio sessions I have lined
Up for during the week." I said.
" You know," She said, " I'm coming to listen
Like it or not because your awesome at music.
Don't even go there."
" Ok I won't go there," I joshed.
" Oh that's it!" she said and started giggling.
I have a date with Freedom." She said.
Freedom was my nickname. I called
Her Love.
As Eagle Hawk I lived a different life
A life of fighting crime.
As Eagle Hawk I was iron.
As Ice Rachael was iron.
We were strong together and fought
The forces of corruption and crime.
As Eagle Hawk I had the ability
To see the world through the eyes of the hawk
I could quickly run. Rachael could throw ice.

Songs of the Black Angels

am   em   am   em7
What we used best was guns.
We lived in a cabin in the mountains
And lived a happy life. Rachael and I
Get to spend our time on earth together.
We loved one another.
" I'm coming to listen," she said again.
I started laughing.
Our first world tour was coming up.
" Oh really," I said.
She started giggling again.
Colorado became my freedom. Starting
My life over there gave me the freedom to
Soar and the freedom to become someone.
As Eagle Hawk I could face the day.
It was through Jesus' forgiveness that
I had become Eagle Hawk. Forgiveness
From a life that led to the grave.
I was Eagle Hawk, a child of Jesus Christ
And the most powerful warrior in the
World. Rachael was my soul mate.

Songs of the Black Angels

We had markings on our bodies.
And we believed that we belonged to a high city.
A holy city. We belonged to Christ.
Rachael and I were in my dreams
And in a river of mercy.
Blood of Christ save us.
Christ is the Lamb of God that
Takes away the sins of the world.
We belonged to a holy order call
The Holy Order of Christ.
There were other orders. This river of mercy flowed.
I never thought when I was younger
That my life could turn out the way it had.
I was Eagle Hawk.
Rachael and I would soon get
Married at Saint Joseph's Catholic Church
In Colorado.
I haven't gotten through life
Without damage. My heart has been
Damaged. Have you ever felt that your nothing?

Songs of the Black Angels

Have friends ever written you off?
It's been enough! I can feel everything
Like a rose. Roses bleed into water.
And I am saved by the rainbow's love.
Rachael and I began life together.
It was a rock star's life.
A life that was waiting for me.
" Do you ever feel like we were
Supposed to meet?" She asked to
Hear the story again. " I feel like we
Are in the hands of destiny. When
I got to Colorado I felt heaven. Colorado
Was a dark paradise for me.
I never knew life could be so beautiful."
The flowers fell in the water.
My life is delicate like flowers in water.
I feel I hold a cup of suffering at times.
How hard is it to get published? How
Would my work get on shelves. Hard work
That's the answer to it all. I had the
Life in Colorado, and I was married to
Someone like an angel. This is
When I thought life had meaning dealing

Songs of the Black Angels

With publishers I felt like life had no
Meaning and quite honestly I find them
Creepy. It doesn't mean that their
On the same side. Someone will
Be. But I make it in the story and
My work gets known.. Rachael was
Everything I wanted in a lover and
More. But who's side am I on
In the story I am on the side of the
Blue collar worker. It has taken
Blood to get somewhere, people can
Be so cold. And maybe it's better
Off that I don't get published
It's been fifteen years. And
Books aren't that great. I'm a
Freedom fighter I came from a long
Line of super heroes and that's
More or less who I am Eagle Hawk.
People on the street know me, but
Business people don't. It's a cold world.
The world has grey clouds in it.
We as people can go our own ways.
Mine is the path of freedom.

Songs of the Black Angels

That's my name Freedom. I stand up
For the truth and I'm going to make
Something out of my life someday.
I walk with heaven.
I believe in heaven.
At the turn of the century, I believed in heaven.
At the end of the day I believe in heaven,
And I pray that God makes straight my path.
Rachael was my lover and best friend.
We were soul mates and I could
Tell this every time we looked
Into each one's eyes. We were
Meant to be together. I got
From Rachael the love I needed.
But there was only one women
For me. Rachael was my destiny.
And so I'm left with the
Questions what about the other
People that I've met and
The answer to that is
Simple they were meant to
Be. Like a priest I would say
Those things were ordained by God.

Songs of the Black Angels

I stay with heaven. I have
Been redeemed by the blood of the
Lamb. I know the hardest thing
Was facing my life of drug addiction
And sorrow, but I have been
Redeemed by the blood of the Lamb
And that has to do with who I
Am not my failures. I am a super hero
And super heroes have pasts. We
Live in a world held up by power and
Greed. And people that don't have a heart beat
And are cold. Life is beautiful
Under the crescent moon.
Life is beautiful, but cold hearted people have kept
The human race down. We are
All in this thing together and life
Is about love. I might not
Go with publishers, and maybe
My work won't end up on a
Dusty shelf. I live
For the eternal flame. There is
More to things than life there is
Eternity.

Songs of the Black Angels

There is good and there is evil.
Two separate paths.
Rachael was good. Christ said
You could judge a tree by it's fruit.
Rachael was good for me. But
The world is no place for
God's children. We are free!
Venus is always close.
Life in Colorado was vastly
Different from how I grew up. I
Am a singer, Rachael is a
Secretary. Singers have powers
So it seems, as super heroes we
Have powers. We live to protect
The common welfare of the people.
All of which brought me to
The place where I was before the cross.
On a Friday night at a book signing.
 Life was promising. Rachael had
Blue eyes. I didn't know a lot of
People with blue eyes. Looking into
Her eyes was like seeing shooting stars.

Songs of the Black Angels

She sat across from me at a
Large table. The book signing had
Gone well. I was living on a large
Piece of property with multiple
Structures. Rachael and I were
In love and that was really
Al I asked for in life. I asked
For her love, that my love
Would be reciprocated. We stayed
Away from criminals. Mayors and cops.
We had our own set of ideals
To judge with. I would put
A product out. Things had to
Get nicer. It was good verses
Evil and a fight to get
Out in the public eye. It meant
Nothing, certainly not to
Compromise one's eternity, but
I had some making up to do.
Some people know me as Israel Kaine
And others know me as Josiah Young.
Israel Kaine is the name I sing under.

Songs of the Black Angels

The fires of heaven that grow hot.
The light shown is from the
Cathedral. My whole life I waited
For someone like Rachael.
" So what are you going to do
If I show up at your studio session?"
" Nothing I can do." " That New Jersey
Accent is cute. I like it. It's sexy."
" It's sexy," I returned.
" Well I'm coming to your gig. Say gig."
" Gig."
" No say it again for reals."
" Gig."
Rachael started laughing at me because I
Was reserved.
" No say it like a professional musician."
" Gig."
Rachael started laughing again.
The times I shared with Rachael
Were beautiful times.
" Say alright." She said.
" Alright."
Rachael started laughing again.

Songs of the Black Angels

Rachael said, " Say water."
" Do we have to play this game where
You laugh at everything I say?"
" Say everything." She played.
We are all energy in the universe.
I began recording Forever in
May of 2011. There were many
Peace keeping groups out along
The streets. Rachael and I
Drove to the studio in the
Foothills and took a room
At the Rabbit Ears Hotel.
Colorado was a beautiful state
With beautiful people.
" Check check. How does this sound,"
Said Josiah. Greg, the recording engineer
Listened.
" That sounds good," said Greg.
" Testing, testing," said Josiah.
" Alright give me some guitar Josiah."
" Ok."

Songs of the Black Angels

I turned up my Stratocaster,
And started playing.
" Is that enough guitar?"
" Yeah you sound fine keep going."
I turned up my Stratocaster.
" That's better," said Greg.
Then I pushed the mic forward.
I put my guitar through cry effects.
I play with Cry Baby effects. Then
I began singing. I was one of
The best singers in the world.
I sang a style of R and B and
Alternative Rock combined. When
I wasn't singing I was doing chant
At the church by my house in upstate New York.
Rachael smiled at me.
I sang about peace and
Love and unity. Crying Buddha
Could make things come into
Alignment when they played. Creation
Became harmonious.
" Testing one two." Josiah that
Sounds good lets hear the
Rest of the band.

Songs of the Black Angels

The band began playing. " Ok keep your levels,"
Said Greg. " You sound fine."
As Eagle Hawk I viewed the world
Differently. Ice and
I were crime fighters and we had friends
In the biz.
Later that evening Rachael and I
Sat in our mansion. We sat
At a large table eating dinner. I was
Rich from music. And Rachael became my confidant.
She became rich when she married me.
" You sounded good today,"
Said Rachael. You sound awesome."
" Thanks," I replied.
" Forever, is going to
Sound good when you all
Get your parts down," Rachael said.
" Thanks," I replied.
" I told you I was going
To come and listen. You
Didn't believe me," Rachael said.

Songs of the Black Angels

" I didn't believe you is rubbish,"
I joked. Rachael started laughing.
" Rubbish?" She asked.
" Plainly." I responded.
Rachael was four years
Older than I. She was
Madly in love with me and
I with her. We would
Spend hours together but it
Got to the point that we
Spent every waking hour
Together. I was living in a
Dream I didn't want to
Wake up from.
" When are you going to record Far Away?"
" We record that next." I said.
" When do you think the crime
Is going to go down?" I said.
" It's always going down," Rachael inferred.
" I agree with you." I said.
" I feel the same about it." I said.
The world was at peace…
" I'm coming for that too. It's
My favorite song." Rachael said.

Songs of the Black Angels

Why life turned out the way it did
I don't know, but it was always getting better.
" When do you think you're going back to work?"
I said. " I don't want to go back. I think
I want to be a groupie." Rachael said.
Her blue eyes were beautiful. She was
A very attractive lady. I loved Rachael
More than words could tell. I wanted
To spend my whole life with her. And
She wanted to spend her whole life with me.
" I feel that the future is promising, Rachael." I said.
" Yes, indeed," she said.
" But you have to love what you're doing.
You love music, don't you. Do you love
What you do hun?" She said. " I love
Music, yes." I said back to her. " You know that,"
I said. " England has to be strong." I said.
" Our political ties should be strengthened
With England."
" England has to stand strong as a nation."
" No, I loved you too." She said.
" Just wait, you always quiet yourself
And shift the focus onto something else.
Just stay." She said.

Songs of the Black Angels

" It doesn't matter Josiah what we have
Or what can be if we don't have
Each other. Don't go away. Don't." She said.
" Life is too short don't." She said.
" I don't know Rachael I've waited
My whole life to get ahead. I just
Don't want to get lost in these circles.
There are so many illusions." I said.
" Just stay and talk that's all
I'm asking you. Just stay."
" That's fine I will."
" So many times I talk and
People don't even listen, but
You're different. You care about others," she said.
" What do you say we do Vegas babes." I said.
" And you get over things easily too.
You're so awesome I love you Josiah." She said.
" What do you say we visit your
Family this weekend." I said.
" My family, don't be ridiculous
We're not going to be up
To visiting. Do you think? She said.

Songs of the Black Angels

" Well it's been awhile." I said.
" Yeah, maybe to the family thing. You
Got me again. Can we please
Maybe love right now." She said.
Then she started laughing.
" I love you Ice," I said.
" And I love you Eagle Hawk," she returned.
" Eagle Hawk don't withdraw. I
Said not to. What do you
Say we stop talking about crime
Fighting and start talking for reals." She said.
I was like "Ah no. Ah no."
The world was Gothic outside.
" We can talk about whatever you
Want to talk about Rachael," I said.
" That's what I like you're getting personal." She said.
" I just think that we spend
Most of our existence crime fighting.
It's clumsy." She said.
" Clumsy. How splendid."
" You're such a bear. That's what
You are, a lovable bear." She said.
" A bear?" I said.
" A bear like yeah." She said.

Songs of the Black Angels

" God like whatever," she said.
" I love my bear." She said.
" See it's nice having you around." She said.
" It's important to take time doing the
Things you love. Well now." I said.
" I know when I came here I was
Looking for other people and I was
Like there's not a lot of people around." I said.
We were Rastafarians. And so
Were our friends.
" I was looking for heads and I
Was like where is everyone. I
Know there's more people around
Than this," I said.
" But it got me thinking," I said.
" It's better to have your brothers
And sisters around." I said.
" Everyone needs people." She said.
" The times in my life when
People aren't around are dark." I said.
" There have been times when
No one has been there." I said.

Songs of the Black Angels

" I know what you mean when I
First came to Colorado from Texas
I didn't know anyone. Those
Were dark times." She said.
" I've had a lot of time to
Think over the years." I said.
" You should be like a Lion from Zion,"
She said. " Be close to the brethren." She said.
" Rachael, I'm just so glad we met.
You are my soul mate. You really
Are." I said.
" I love you Josiah Young." She
Said in return.
I thought a lot about things.
The world was dark and unjust. It was
A cruel world. What I needed more
Than anything was love. And Rachael
Gave me that and I her.
The world was dark outside.
There was a phoenix that rose
Through the clouds.
" Well, I'm glad we had this chat." I said.

Songs of the Black Angels

" So am I," said Rachael.
" When I first came out to Colorado
There were like no people like us around.
I finally came across some Rastafarians
In the area." She said.
" I just wish away the world." She said.
" I want to live close to people,
I want to be part of a bigger thing.
But Josiah the world is a hard place
To live in. It's cold how people are
Treated." She said.
" That it is." I said in return.
There were dark blue clouds in the sky.
" You know, it's hard being an artist
In this world. It sets you apart." I said.
" That it does." She said.
Rachael passed some food across
The table and upped her wine.
" Salute." I responded.

Songs of the Black Angels

" You know we were meant for each other."
Rachael said.
" I'm a full believer that we're soul mates.
I just want to get closer to you Siah."
" And I you," I said in response.
Rachael had blue eyes and long, thick
Black dreadlocks. I had dreadlocks
Too but being into music my hairstyle
Would change.
" You know being Rastafarian separates
You apart from other people. True
Rastafarians believe Haile Selassie was
The second coming of Christ, but
None of us Rastafarians believe this.
Your Rasta if you believe in the good."
Out in the world it was good versus evil.
For some it had always been that way.
" Your Rasta if you believe in the
Good," I responded.
" Just don't clam up and go
Away. Stay with me talking. I
Love you. I want you to be comfortable
And for you to be yourself. Loosen up around me."
Rachael said.

Songs of the Black Angels

" I talked to Mr. Stone, the record
Producer he says we should go
With an Indie label." I said.
" Well Mr. Stone has been in the business
For a long time he has quite a
Background. Did he say why he feels
That way. that you should go with
An Indie label." Rachael said.
" He feels that we could keep things
The way they are with an Indie label.
He feels that since we have ten
Members in the band that that doesn't
Look good for us." I said.
" Well listen to Mr. Stone but
He is not Saint Peter here." Rachael said.
" No, Mr. Stone is not Saint Peter." I said.
" Mr. Stone is a good man. Crying Buddha
Appreciates his work." I responded.
" Just don't go away." Rachael
Stood up and spun like a dancer.
She was wearing a long white dress.
Rachael sat back down at the table.

Songs of the Black Angels

" I work too hard for the treatment." I said.
" As a singer I work very hard but
There's a lot of people in the music
Business." I said.
" Josiah stay and talk to me, your
Always on the go. Would you just
Stay with me and talk." She said.
" Yeah, but I can tell you're not going
To take that long."
" I'm here, I'll talk." I said.
" Yaey. I got you to myself." Rachael's
Eyes filled up with tears.
" You got me all to yourself." I said.
I could feel her love. Her love was
In my heart. I loved her more than
Words could tell.
" Josiah I love you so much," Rachael
Started crying.
" Do you believe me," she said.
" I believe you." I said.

Songs of the Black Angels

" Do you know since we got married
It's been like a dream." Rachael said.
" I love you so much." Said Rachael.
" And I love you." I said to her.
Josiah our intimate moments
Mean something to me. That's why
I said stay because this is intimacy
And we're married." Rachael said.
There was a picture of us in the mansion.
When Rachael had long, blonde hair.
Falcon Crest stood on a tall building.
A rich couple walked home
From the theater and two
Robbers approached them. They had
Guns. Falcon Crest swooped down
And webbed the two burglars.
He hit the guns from their hands.
He had to intervene because the
Couple was going to get robbed.
Falcon Crest called to the police and
Swooped away.

Songs of the Black Angels

Josiah had special powers and
Was a singer. He could tell when
Significant things were happening. He
Was very empathetic.
Josiah looked at Rachael his
Young wife. She had her nose ring in.
" Just! Don't stop like I said before
Stay and talk that's what
We're doing. Other people may be
Doing other things. But this is
What we're doing. There's two of us
In the relationship, not one so
Don't leave me."
" I won't," Josiah said.
" Now where's the weed." Rachael said.
Rachael and I started laughing.
Catman shut off the lights in
His house.
" You're not Eagle Hawk and I'm not
Ice right now people need to have
Lives. Things happen out there."

Songs of the Black Angels

Washington was a grey cloud.
The world was covered with darkness.
Mars, that dark red ball.
I started to hear the music again.
Before life was pain again and again.
I did nothing to deserve it.
Sometimes good people feel pain.
I would write for a women.
That's where things add up for me.
I write for her.
This soul chooses peace.
Not machine guns.
And that's what makes
Me different from others.
Someday life will add up.
And I'll beat the publishing companies.
I don't want them anyway.
It does no justice.
I'm one person in a big world.
I'm a writer for today.
But I will.
I don't have a chip on my shoulders.

Songs of the Black Angels

I would rather start chain saws.
Or shoot Oozies.
Then sit here and think of cocaine
An endless stream of cigarettes.
Beware of the cobras.
You can called me Viper.
I'm a runaway.
The tropical orange scene is
Filled with black and white people.
The TV's are black and white .
Life can't reach one through
The TV, I'm not taking calls.
I'm putting my faith in an audience
An audience that doesn't
Care about publishers and injustice.
My work will get out
Because it should.
I have no idea
What the fuck do I look like
A clone or something.
I don't talk to horses
What the fuck?
You can't even use the f word
With some of these guys.

Songs of the Black Angels

They have so many people
Kissing their asses.
I will put myself with good
Companies and good people.
That's just the way the mandolin plays.
I don't like publishing companies
I have yet to read a good book.
My sisters say I'm a trip.
And you're listening to a trip with
What do people like, trips.
Stay away from the Abilify I'm hanging fuck it
Have your Abilify I talk to myself too much.
The fire birds fly in a vacant sky.
Breaking.
These are break beats.
Poetry whities poetry whities.
The whities the publishing companies
Who brought them into this circle?
I stay away from cocaine.
Forget about it.

Songs of the Black Angels

I don't need them.
I have my eyes on Porsche.
Don't underestimate God.
You'll have the Christian companies
Supporting language.
Say it doesn't even make sense,
Here's to you who made it somewhere.
Now I just have to get to Sigourney Weaver's house.
You dance with the fucking Devil.
No you sugar.
Dam how would you like to he her.
She's on fire.
She's on fire, fire, fire.
The sun is yellow and red.
I'm just trying to be friendly.
I'll stay away from those Cubans.

Songs of the Black Angels

I saw my first shining star when
I was eighteen.
Fair market trade call is what you want.
A panther walks at the dead of night.
The world Chico.
This s- is bad to the bone.
What are you accusing me of.
That's a killing and I'm a customer.
If you are going to listen to them
Start priming.
White paint thanks.
It works better than black.
You know what I mean.
You don't need them.
Watch what you support.
With your wallet thanks.
Scar face will be back after
These messages.
I believe in health.
This town is great.
My own boat.
My own golf course.
And no Cubans.

Songs of the Black Angels

The skies are blue.
I want to run in strawberry fields.
We dance with flowers.
My Cadillac looks like someone's
Nightmare.
But books, I want to get married.
45,000 fully equipped
That or the machine gun
I'm bored
45,000 fully equipped
I like you better
The walking dead
I am a living machine.
What is important is being
Close to Jesus.
Prejudice is wrong.
Love is like thunder.
The skies are grey.
I dream of the day I make it.
Falcon Crest walks along
The buildings.

Songs of the Black Angels

" Josiah you're a child of light." She said.

" And so are you Rachael Ray." I replied. Her nickname.

" Josiah you know how much you mean to me."

Rachael and I sat at the table.

" I don't know what I would do without you." She said.

" I love you too." I said.

" Being Rasta is staying

True to the faith that God

Loves you. It's not believing Haile Selassie was the

Second coming of Christ."

I said.

" You can believe what

You want to believe." I said.

" Being real is

Being real." I said.

" People say being Rasta

Means you believe Haile

Selassie was the second coming

Of Christ. That's not necessarily

True." Said Rachael.

Songs of the Black Angels

" Being Rasta is believing
True things," said Rachael.
" Being Rasta is believing
True things. It doesn't hinge
On Haile Selassie being the
Second coming of Christ." I said.
And so at times one has to
Part from the world.
" Being Rasta is believing
In hemp I can say that." I said.
" Using hemp is important." Rachael said.
" But saying your Rasta because
You believe Haile Selassie was the second
Coming of Christ is not." Rachael said.
" It's more than eating
at Rasta Pasta." I said.
" Josiah stay and talk with me
Don't go away." Said Rachael.
" Josiah I want to tell you
Something and I don't know how
You're going to take it." Said Rachael.

Songs of the Black Angels

" What is it?" I said.
" I still love you." Rachael said.
" That was it." Rachael said.
" I love you too." I said.
Rachael and I were Rastafarians.
We believed being Rastafarian had
To do with belief and living the
Truth. We believed it had to do with being
Kind to living creatures.
Others believed it was
Believing Haile Selassie was the second
Coming of Christ. We believed
It was being kind to others.
" Rachael having you in my
Life doesn't escape me. I love you
Very much." I said.
Rachael put her hair back.
Harvest Moon played on an old radio.
" I love having you in my life," I said to
Rachael.
" I feel the same way," she said in return.

Songs of the Black Angels

" Do you think we should reduce
The crime fighting," I asked.
" Josiah just stay here and talk. Don't
Go out crime fighting. We were meant
To be together and we should be.
But don't walk out that door." Rachael said.
The news was on TV, but no one
Was in the room to listen.
" It was destiny that we met. Good
Kindred are meant to be together." I said.
" There are stories on TV
About crime fighting. Just leave it go."
" That's fine Rachael," I said in response.
Rachael and I were newly married.
She was a beautiful person. I was happy
With her. And she was happy with me.
" I feel like there are angels
around us." I said.
" So do I," Rachael said.
" Just stay and talk with me.
Forget about the rest." Said Rachael.

Songs of the Black Angels

" We'll stay and talk," I said to her.
" Angels with white wings are all
Around us," I said.
" The things in this world
That cause separation
From God are evil." Rachael said.
" We were meant to be together so
You're going to stay and talk." Said Rachael.
" Who is Rastafari." Said Rachael.
" Rastafari is God as man." I said.
" But Haile Selassie was some general." I said.
" Being Rastafarian is being kind
To living creatures. Some say it's
Believing Haile Selassie was the second
Coming of Christ. But he was
Some general." I said in return.
I was a singer and Rachael was
A secretary. I was famous
And wealthy. After Rachael married
Me she came into the money.
We were super heroes, but we were
Taking time off and spending time
With one another. In the midst of it all.

Songs of the Black Angels

" Some say I'll be in my saviors
Arms," I said.
" Me too," Rachael said.
" Loving Jesus is like a crimson ocean,"
I said.
" Loving Jesus is like a yellow ocean,"
Rachael said.
" God is close to you Josiah," Rachael said.
" And the same for you," I said.
" God led us together," I said to Rachael.
" That's what I'm saying Josiah, we
Were meant to be together," Rachael said.
" I love you," I said to Rachael.
" Rastafarians are different people. Their
Their own tribe." Rachael said.
" Rastafarians long to be with God, they
Long to be with each other. Kindred should
Be together." Rachael said.
" Rastafarians are good people. That
Live their lives by love. They love the
Environment. They are globally conscious.
The list goes on and on and on." Josiah
Young said.

Songs of the Black Angels

" People associate Rastafarians with
Drugs, but the truth is real Rastafarians
Are against violence and prejudice.
They're a good people." Said Rachael.
" It's hard to say if God walked as
Man, some people
Base things off of this." Said Josiah Young.
Jah is a word for God." Said Rachael.
" We say Jah for God." Said Rachael.
" Rastafarians are peace loving." Said Josiah.
There was Rastafarians around
Colorado and they used to frequent
The studio. Crying Buddha was known
As " good people."
Josiah and Rachael sat in their
Mansion talking. The world was in
A time of peace.
" Jesus is the Lamb of God," Josiah said.
" The Father loves us," said Rachael.
Rachael was my soul mate. We
Loved each other.

Song of the Blue Skies

" The world has never really recognized
Rastafarians. But they are their own people."
Rachael said.
A cross hung in the room.
There was a stone crucifix. Light
From the stain glass came inside.
In the stain glass a dove was in the sky.
" They are their own people," said Josiah.
" Our roots are not in Jamaica they
Are here in America." Said Rachael.
" it is important to stay with your roots,"
said Rachael.
" Rachael I love you." I said.
" I love you Josiah." Rachael said.
There was a silver heart
On a dove in the stain glass.
A picture of Jesus in the garden
Of Gethsemane.
There were doves with silver hearts.
The mansion was quiet except
For Josiah and Rachael's voices.

Songs of the Black Angels

" Do you want some Rum Raisin
Ice cream. It's very good." Rachael said.
" I know I bought it." Josiah laughed.
" I thought I would offer you your
Ice cream. It's good." Rachael said.
Time is an eternity when your
In love, and you always wish to be
On time's side.
Rachael and Josiah had found one
Another in the midst of life's struggles.
They had come together.
" Do you remember when we used
To date. You used to advise me on
My food." Josiah said.
" That's because you buy good food." Said Rachael.
" I'm glad I can advise you on it." Rachael
Said sarcastically. " I sounded
Like you when I said that." Rachael said.
" It's important to be who you
Are," Rachael said.
" You're going to do well in life." She said.

Songs of the Black Angels

" So do you want some of the Rum Raisin," Rachael said.
" Yeah, give me some," said Josiah.
" The night I met you , I saw my first
Shining star." Said Rachael.
" That's how I knew you were the one." Said Rachael.
" I saw shooting stars on our first
Three dates as well. As if
One shooting star wasn't enough." Said Rachael.
" When we first dated I felt a certain peace.
Kind of like how I felt on the wedding
Night." Said Rachael.
" Stick with the rum ice cream kid. You
Got an older women here." Rachael said.
Rachael was older.
Falcon Crest stood over the city.
" I'm a stud what can I say." Said Josiah.
" A stud? For nailing a chick like me.
Shoot." Rachael said.
" Nailing?" Josiah said.
" Nailing you expect me to take that?"
Josiah said. Rachael began laughing again.

Songs of the Black Angels

" I love you." She said again.
" Josiah, you must think I'm a
Hopeless Romantic I can't believe you
Get me in these moods I just want
To say where's the weed." Rachael
Laughed. Josiah laughed too.
" Listen Josiah we're married you
Can stay and talk to me. Tell
Me how you kicked marijuana
Again."
" Well matter of fact, I'll tell
You." Josiah said.
" Well, what about me." Rachael said.
" I used to be an addict. Then
I asked for forgiveness and I became
Eagle Hawk. Josiah said.
" Josiah there are others like you.
Shoot what about alcohol? Many
Super heroes have a past." Rachael said.
" The originals are the originals.
In different generations different
Things happened. There's no formula."
Said Rachael.

Songs of the Black Angels

" I love you." She said again.
" Josiah, you must think I'm a
Hopeless Romantic I can't believe you
Get me in these mood I just want
To say where's the weed." Rachael
laughed. Josiah laughed too.
" Listen Josiah we're married you
Can stay and talk to me. Tell
Me how you kicked marijuana
Again."
" Well matter of fact, I'll tell
You." Josiah said.
" Well, what about me." Rachael said.
" I used to be an addict. Then
I asked for forgiveness, and I became
Eagle Hawk. Josiah said.
" Josiah there are others like you.
Shoot what about alcohol? Many
Super heroes have a past." Rachael said.
" The originals are the originals.
In different generations different
Things happened. There's no formula."
Said Rachael.

Songs of the Black Angels

The rest of the mansion was quiet.
" Josiah you have a gift. You inspire
Me." Rachael said.
" Thanks," said Josiah.
" Thanks," Rachael poked. " Let me hear
That New Jersey accent." She laughed.
" And lead guitar. You're very gifted." Said Rachael.
" Josiah we have to seize these
Moments. Don't ever give up. You'll
Make it." Said Rachael.
" These past months I've wondered
If I would make it as a singer. I
Thought about losing my voice and
How hard that was. Being a
Singer is a challenging occupation."
Josiah said.
" You're telling me, a secretary. Oh
Forget about it." Rachael said.

Songs of the Black Angels

" One more for crime fighting." Josiah said.
" And here's to crime fighting." Rachael
Lifted up her champagne to toast.
Rachael and Josiah toasted.
" Rachael Ray I love you," Josiah
Laughed.
Rachael laughed in return.
" Rachael Young is fine." She said.
Rachael was new age, but not pagan.
Roses bled into the fountain.
The water was calm and serene.
Their voices echoed in the mansion.
" I like my new name Young," Rachael replied.
" I'm sure you do," laughed Josiah.
Rachael made eyes at him.
" Listen Rachael we are very fortunate
We have so much in life we should
Donate." Josiah said.
" Honey your bachelor days are
Far from over." She laughed.
" Ah, no. That was a bummer.
Selfless servitude over hea."

Songs of the Black Angels

" Donating is fine," she said.
The mansion grew dark.
" Josiah light some candles honey,
I'm tired of babysitting what's the deal?"
" What do you mean," said Josiah.
" I mean it's getting dark and we
Usually go out crime fighting. But we're
Married. And it's good for a change to stay in."
Said Rachael.
" I refer to Whitney as Trilogy Heart,
It is his nickname." Said Josiah.
" Trilogy Heart is the nickname
He earned crime fighting." Said Josiah.
" Saint Michael will protect us," said Josiah.
" Saint Michael will protect us," Rachael said.
" Josiah do you know that you
Mean so much to me." Rachael said.
" I love you Rachael," said Josiah.
They toasted again.
There was a stone cross outside.

Songs of the Black Angels

" Josiah you know that
When we met I knew
You were special," Rachael said.

God the Son,
Redeemer of the world.

Morning star pray for us.
" Josiah something is going to happen
In your life that will confirm you
Are special and it could have
Been you getting into Crying Buddha."
Said Rachael.
" I believe it was when I got
Into Crying Buddha." Said Josiah.
" So do I," Rachael said.
" Crying Buddha is a deep gig," Rachael said.
" It means you are who you are,"
Rachael said.
" But Rachael you care about me. There
Is no one in the whole world that
Loves me the way you do." Josiah said.

Songs of the Black Angels

" I have passion for you Josiah.
You're safe with me." Rachael said.
" I love you," Josiah said.
" We're going to make it
And everything is going to be
Alright we don't have to be
Out crime fighting." Rachael said.
" I believe that," Josiah said.
" Always believe," Rachael said.
" When you write it all
Comes together. Stay with it.
And keep writing." Rachael said.
" That way you can get studio gigs."
Rachael said.
" I will keep writing and
Composing," Josiah said.
There was a statue of Mary.
Josiah's house was a lair.

Outside waves hit the shores of
The lake.
" Josiah you have to promise
Me something," Rachael said.
" I want you to promise me
That you'll never give up Hun,
Will you do that for your bear."
Rachael said.

Songs of the Black Angels

" I will promise." Josiah responded.
" All we have are these moments.
Time falls through our hands. Nothing
Can buy love. Do you catch
My drift." Rachael said.
" Yes," Josiah said.
" Like grains in an hour glass." Josiah said.
" But Josiah we were meant to
Be together," Rachael said.
" Do you believe that?"
" Yes, yes I do." Said Josiah.
We were Rastas, kindred. We were
Our own people. There was a hope
Like no other. Being a singer fueled
Something within me.
" You're either Rasta and you're
In or you're not Rasta and you're out." Josiah said.
If you were Rasta you believed in good.
You ate organic food, you listened to Reggae.
Rachael said, " If you're Rasta you
Believe in the good. And you
Live out what you believe."

Songs of the Black Angels

" Rachael," Josiah said," Who were
You before you became a super hero?"
" I was a petite secretary who
Did nothing but read. When I became
Ice I stood within God's glory."
Rachael said.
Josiah said, " So when did you get your
Own unicorn."
" I got my own unicorn after
I became Ice." Said Rachael.
" When did you get yours," said Rachael.
" I got my first unicorn when I became
Eagle Hawk. I have two unicorns
Sage Water and Crescent Moon. I got my
Second one shortly after." Said Josiah.
The voices in the mansion boomed.
" Our anniversary is coming up,"
Josiah said.
" That it is," said Rachael.
" May 04,[th] said Josiah.

Songs of the Black Angels

" You know the mayor hasn't been in
These parts in quite some time. Stopped
Coming around," Said Rachael.
" Corrupt government officials don't
Sail in these parts." Josiah said.
" And neither do the cops." Said Rachael.
" Josiah I want you to know
That I love you." Rachael said.
" You know that don't you," Rachael said.
" Yes, very much," said Josiah Young.
" You can call me Rachael Young,
I like it better." Said Rachael.
" You and the Cartoon Network. You're
Adorable." Rachael said.
" I've taken a beating over the
Last few months crime fighting." Josiah said.
" I know but we're not going to talk
About it. Remember I said no
Crime fighting." Rachael said.
" It's just us tonight," Said Rachael.
" Just us." Josiah said.
" Well yeah," said Rachael.

Songs of the Black Angels

Josiah said, " People say that Rastafarians
Believe their marijuana is the body of Christ.
But not all Rastafarians are like that."
Josiah Young said, " Rastafarians believe in
Hemp, they believe in natural things and
Organic things, but there are a lot of
Misconceptions about Rastafarians in
Reference to their practices. Rastafarians
Believe in hemp."
Rachael said, " Using hemp has a
Global impact it's a New Age belief."
" It's like eating clams."
Josiah and Rachael laughed.
Josiah was wearing his warm-up suit.
Rachael was wearing a dress.
There were dressed as Josiah and
Rachael Young, not as super heroes.
" I love you." Josiah said.
" I love you too," said Rachael.
Josiah was a music artist.
" You have to look out for yourself."
Josiah said.

Songs of the Black Angels

Rachael said with tears in her eyes," Yeah
I guess I do."
" What's more important is us.
Not the revolution not crime fighting, us."
A cross hung from the ceiling in the
Room.
Candles flickered.
Josiah looked at the newspapers
Filled with crime and then look away.
Rachael said, " Ok I know how
It is. It's us. Two people that
Are in love."
There were flowers outside.
" Rastafarians believe in hemp they
Believe in practical things. Things that
Are good for the environment.
Rachael had long black dreadlocks
And a nose ring. Josiah had
A tattoo that said Rachael and was
Crossed out and another tattoo that
Said Rachael. There was no
Significance, just what it meant
To have someone's name tattooed on
Your arm. Josiah thought the first was practice.
No significance though.

Songs of the Black Angels

" Nice tattoo," said Rachael.
Josiah laughed.
Josiah said, " Rastafarians believe
That love is a fundamental belief that
Your life is based on love."
Rachael agreed with him.
Josiah said, " Things have to be
Organic if you're going to use them."
Rachael nodded her head.
" I don't like the gods, alright."
He hit his fist to the table.
When the bad guys win
The good guys lose. Basic.
How many people do we have in
Jails." Josiah said.
Rachael looked at Josiah. " Josiah
I love you," she said with tears in her
Eyes."
" And I love you." Said Josiah.

Songs of the Black Angels

Two young lovers.

Sun filled streams.
" What people have to do in this
World is unrealistic. Crime… forget about it
There is crime in everything. Everything you
Pick up…" Josiah said. Angels played
On burning violins.
" What this is about is Bank Robbers."
Said Josiah.
" Josiah I asked for a change
You wouldn't bring it up, but your
Right. Ok your right. You usually are."
Said Rachael.
" I am," said Josiah.
The church bell rang. Lightning flashed
Outside.
There was the sound of violins.
But everything was not ok.
These conversations were common for people
To have during the Revolution.

Songs of the Black Angels

There were angels with M-16's. One angel
Threw a lighter that was lit. Fire spread.

" Being Rastafarian is believing in
The good of creation and believing in hemp." Said Josiah Young.
There were microphones off on the side
Of a room.
" I'm Rasta Josiah. You're Rasta.
How are people like us going to
Survive?" Said Rachael.
The revolution is important, but
It's not everything this is what
We have. Don't compromise what
We have." Said Rachael.
The sound of a piano played outside
In a Gothic world. Rose pedals fell
From roses in the mansion.
" No matter how much you change
You have to pay the price of your actions regardless."
Said Josiah.
Like roses bleeding in the sky.

Songs of the Black Angels

" If you see something, say something it's
Basic Josiah. Now you got me talking,
But I'm not giving into it." Said Rachael.
" It's a new world. New Zion. Come on
Take a load off." Said Rachael.
" New Zion," said Josiah.
Diamonds were written in the sky.
The young mountains rolled.
" Rachael who are your angels?"
" He's jealous. Who?
Josiah started laughing and so did Rachael.
" What?" Said Rachael.
" What's the big deal," said Rachael.
" Some Rastafarians believe that Haile Selassie
Was the second coming of Christ
Others do not. They believe that he was
Chosen by God and is their earthly king.
But there are those who believe that
Rasta is about the earth. And holistic
Medicines and culture. Home cooking."
Said Rachael Ray.
" But Babylon is western culture. And
Babylon makes the rules." Said Josiah Young.
" Africa may be the birth place of mankind."
Said Rachael.
" There are prophets that have risen
Over the years." Said Josiah.

Songs of the Black Angels

" John 14:2 says that there are many
Rooms in my father's house." Josiah said.
" The Niyabinghi drumming is an
enormous influence in my music."
Said Josiah Young.
" My music is influenced by
The recording studio and definitive sound."
Said Josiah Young.
" I want to make music movies. Movies that have music
As the main element. " Said Josiah.
" But being a Recording Artist is
Something that I work at day in and day out."
Said Josiah.
" The studio is a place where the magic
Happens. And you can record. Pro Tools
Is good equipment. But nothing takes the
Place of my Fender Stratocaster."
Said Josiah.
" Lead guitar is sacred. And writing
Guitar solos is a large part of my
Compositions."
" Piano is important too."
" But my music is influenced by Africa
Tremendously. And also by Reggae. So
Therefore the Rasta movement is
Important to mention with Reggae music also."
" Reggae music is influenced by the Rasta movement."
Said Josiah Young.

" Reggae sounds very Native American."
Said Josiah. " But Haile Selassie was
An earthly ruler. And Rasta has different
Components. Organic is a component.
Holistic medicine perhaps. Respecting life."
" Saying Haile Selassie is the second
Coming of Christ is a worldly belief.
You can be Rasta and not believe Haile Selassie
Was the second coming of Christ or is your
Early king. Rastafari is a movement
That adheres to nature and the earth. And
Rasta women cook well." Said Josiah Young.

Songs of the Black Angels

" Nor does one have to use cannabis spiritually.
In Switzerland cannabis is legal for use of incense.
California has legalized cannabis for medicinal use.
And so has Colorado. Cannabis is legal in
Amsterdam. But it's a plant. Rastafarians
Believe different things. It is an earth ideology."
" That's why we celebrate Earth Day."
" Citrus is important in food. Medicine."
" 1949 the Geneva Conventions are important
In a political sense. But being Rasta is being
Rasta. It's earth based. Natural. And good
Food." Said Josiah.
" Let's not get into the religion." Said Josiah.
" But Josiah we're alive. People love one
Another." Said Rachael Ray.
" We have to live life to the fullest."
Said Rachael Ray.
" Reggae is a way to celebrate life." Said Rachael.
" Let's not get into marijuana." Said Rachael.
" Straight Edge is the way to go." Said Josiah.
Straight Edge means no alcohol and no drugs.
" Diversity is important." Said Josiah.
" Surely Haile Selassie is not Christ. You
Can still be Rasta. Babylon makes the rules
And people suffer." Said Josiah.

Songs of the Black Angels

" Jah lives." Said Josiah.
" Jah is ever living." Said Josiah.
" Jah is a father. If you know
Your heavenly father loves you
You feel happy inside. You feel
Accepted and loved. That's what
Is important. To know that you are
Loved by Jah. We should raise
Our children to know our
Heavenly father. People need
God's love. They need Jah. Celebrating
Is a large part of life. We celebrate life
Because we love life. We love being
Alive. Smelling the fresh air and
The flowers. The earth is a garden.
And it's as though there are angels before
The Garden of Eden though we are
Loved by Jah and are with Jah all the
Time. Jah makes us happy inside.
He fills us with love. And we have
Love for one another. That's why
We say Hallelujah. Because our
Heavenly father loves us." Said Josiah.

Songs of the Black Angels

The night was black crystal by then.
" My life is music. Reggae is a large
Part of my life." Said Josiah.
" I remember when I went into
The music studio my first time, things
Just clicked. Reggae celebrates life and our
Heavenly father." Said Josiah.
" Our heavenly father loves us." Said Josiah.
" He is worthy of our praise." Said Josiah.
Rachael said, " We are part of a revolution
As earth rises before the wicked."
Rachael said, " Our heavenly father loves us.
Hallelujah. I'll praise your name."
" We are meant to live together." Rachael said.
" I tried to satisfy the hunger." Said Josiah.
" But there is a burning desire." Said Josiah.
" Not everything is lost. We have our innocence." Said Josiah.
" My heart is singing." Said Josiah.
" Jah's love conquers all." Said Josiah.
" All I ever needed was God's love." Said Josiah.
" Jesus, worthy is the Lamb that was slain for us."
Said Rachael.
" We are the people of the Rastafarian movement. We
Are Rastas. The revolution stretches on." Said Rachael.
" God has his hand on us." Said Rachael.
" All the world will praise his great name." Said Josiah.
There were unicorns of ceramic dancing.
Maria
" Jah says 'I will show my love to the world.'" Said Josiah.
Golden Cobras
" Jah is love praise his name." Said Josiah.
" Jah is love," said Rachael.

Songs of the Black Angels

" Jah lives." Said Josiah.
Mercy
God's Mercy endures forever
" Jah lives." Said Rachael.
" Reggae is about God's love. Some
Believe that it's praise music. Not
everyone."
" Your Rasta if you love God and
Love others." Said Josiah.
" Josiah we are so young we have
Such a promising future. We're going
To make it." Said Rachael.
" But the music… the music has
To make it. How is our music going
To make it." Said Josiah.
" Your music is electricity." Said Rachael.
" There's a place where you belong. And
That's behind your instrument." Said Rachael
" Lead guitar is important."
" Communication is like flowers. You have
To have it." Said Rachael.
" And our spirits respond in many ways and
To many things." Said Rachael.
" You're Rasta because you say your
Rasta. Not because you believe Haile Selassie
Was the second coming of Christ. Haile Selassie
Was man. Not God incarnate. Rastas are more
Than that." Said Rachael.
" Rasta is not even religion it's culture." Said Rachael.

Songs of the Black Angels

" We're all one unified family. People
Were meant to live together." Said Rachael.
" Our heavenly father deserves our praise."
Said Josiah.
" Is it too late to learn?" Said Josiah.
" No it's not." Said Rachael.
" It's never too late to learn." Said Rachael.
" We should cast out the shadows of our fears."
Said Josiah.
" There is no fear in love." Said Rachael.
" Hallelujah," said Josiah.
" Jah lives." Said Rachael.
" The Black Cobras protect us." Said Josiah.
" God sends his angels." Said Josiah.
" God loves us." Said Josiah.
" We shouldn't run from God." Said Rachael.
" There nothing that you've done that
Separates us from the love of God." Said Rachael.
" God is with us." Said Josiah.
" God loves us." Said Rachael.
" Give me wings to fly. This is more
Than I can do. I'm strong enough. But
it's like I'm fallen. It's like I'm fallen."
" Fallen in love." Said Rachael.
" I'm awakened knowing God's love."
Said Josiah.
" Jesus is the messiah." Said Rachael.
" God is holy." Said Josiah.
" Praise God. Praise God." Said Rachael.
These are the lyrics of the Black Angels.
" God is holy." Said Josiah.

Songs of the Black Angels

" The shadows scattered when
You are there." Said Josiah.
" You are like love Rachael."
" Praise God." Said Rachael.
" God deserves our worship. Not Hail Selassie."
Said Rachael.
" We are in the Father's heart," said Josiah.
Rachael said, " The sun shines with
His glory."
Rachael said, " When the darkness surrounds us
God's love is near."
" Blessed be the name of the Lord." Said Josiah.
" Flows the glory of his name." Said Josiah.
" You are the Morning Star." Said Josiah.
" You are the Morning Glory." Said Josiah.
" Being Rasta means that you believe in
Natural things. Not that Haile Selassie was
The second coming of Christ, or that he is
An earthly king."
" You can still be Rasta if it's part of who
You are."
" Because of your love we're forgiven."
Said Josiah.
" Your love is far reaching." Said Rachael.
" You are a star Jesus. The incarnate son.
To all the underserving. You promises
Are help that is on the way." Said Josiah Young.
" When I learned with my life, of
Your love. I was released from the cold."
Said Josiah Young.
" Help is on the way. He will save the day."
Beautiful son. We're going far.
" When help is on the way. He will save the day."
You are beautiful, my sweet song.
" You are so good."
" You are healing."

Songs of the Black Angels

You are my song.
" I will sing to God all
My days. You poured out
Your Blood."
" You are my Jesus."
" Have you been searching.
Have you felt all the things
That are empty. There is
More than gold in your hands.
Have you been looking for
Forgiveness and rest."
 Let it fade."
" I have seen what this world
Has to offer." Said Josiah.
Let it fade."
You are my song.
You carried the weight
Of the cross.
" You can rest.
You who are
Heavy laden. "
" Let it fade."
" My whole life can crumble…"
Said Josiah.
" Are you looking for a
river to call home." Said Rachael.
" We will follow God." Said Rachael.
" Black Cobras are entwined."
" I want my stereo."
" We cry holy."

Songs of the Black Angels

" God is holy." Said Josiah.
" Holy is the Lamb." Said Josiah.
" The unicorns ride." Said Rachael.
" I want my stereo." Said Josiah.
" From my stereo is a sweet sound." Said Josiah.
" As far as the eye can see. Never
Fade away." Said Josiah.
" You shine." Said Josiah.
" Jesus is the Lamb." Said Josiah.
" I love your more than
The things in this world." Said Josiah.
" I will not let go." Said Josiah.
" The glory of the sun will not fade." Said Josiah.
" The glory of the sun will not fade." Said Josiah.
" I love God. God is holy." Said Josiah.
" You are a light that saves." Said Josiah.
" You are the Lamb that was
Slain." Said Rachael.
" You lead the way." Said Josiah.
Solo. " You saved us
From the grey clouds, that
Fell from the dark sky.
You saved us from the grey
Clouds, that bound us."
" Jesus you light the way." Said Rachael.
" Turn the stereo on. This is for
The hour of the Christians, who
Came before us. Who failed
Where we had to succeed.
The grey clouds surround us.
You are a light that saves."
" Jesus is the light that saves." Said Rachael.
" I am alive again." Said Josiah.

Songs of the Black Angels

Solo.
" I want the world to know that
You are the light that saves."
" You carried the cross and
We are saved. I am alive again.
You are the origins of our faith."
" I belong to you. I've been searching
For a place of my own. Why this
World holds us. While you do
Miracles that save."
" You are the miracles that save."
" You are the light that saves."
" After all my searching,
You lead me to the light."
" You are the Lamb."
" We dance in streets that
Are gold." Josiah said.
Solo. " This is a message,
That the Gospel saves the
World. And you are
A merciful exchange."
" Wars fall like destiny."
" You are there when we
Breathe.
You are a merciful exchange."
" Life doesn't always come
Easy. Trying to put the pieces together."
" Your sweet sound."
" God you are our sweet sound."
" I got nothing good. Just bills to pay."

Songs of the Black Angels

" God you are eternity."
" God you are our shelter."
" I have lived in the shadows
Of shame. But you have been there
For me."
" I'm yours."
Ceramic unicorns fly.
Born and remains.
Born and remain.
" I look up to number one." Said Josiah.
" Everywhere we go, God
Is with us. I just want to
Be closer to God." Said Rachael.
" To know that God is close." Said Rachael.
Ceramic unicorns are born.
Beautiful love in drops of sun.
The glory of the sun never fades.
As this love is strong like Cobras.
" I've been a dreamer. You
Are the redeemer. Christ." Said Josiah.
Ceramic unicorns stay alive.
I lift my hands.
To rejoice.
" God is the redeemer." Said Josiah.

" Shadows fall." Said Josiah.
" God is always with us." Said Rachael.

" God has redeemed our souls." Said Rachael.
" The glory of the cross..." Said Rachael.
" Jah lives children." Said Rachael.

Songs of the Black Angels

" God's glory never fades." Said Josiah.

" God has rescued us from the grave." Said Rachael.

" God is wonderful." Said Josiah.

" Cobras encircle." Said Rachael.

" God has given us love." Said Josiah.

" We speak through songs." Said Rachael.

" What God means to us." Said Josiah.

" You redeem us." Said Rachael Ray.

" Here I am again. Worshiping you." Said Josiah.

" Always searching. Crashing at the surface.
Become alive. God picks me up to his wings.
Forgiveness and rest." Said Josiah.

" You're the only one." Said Rachael.

"Don't leave me." Said Josiah.

" You're willing to fight." Said Rachael.

" Don't leave me." Said Josiah.

" I'm willing to fight. For
Tomorrow." Said Rachael.

" This is gold." Said Josiah.

" All the hours that go by." Said Josiah.

" Spread our wings to fly." Said Josiah.

" In the river space and time." Said Josiah.

" God loves us like crimson gold." Said Rachael.

" God is with us." Said Rachael.

Solo. " And you love me as I am."

" You always will and you always do."

" God loves us." Josiah Young.

" God loves us." Josiah Young.

" Don't leave me." Rachael said.

" I never will. I will always love you."
Josiah said.

" Praise God." Rachael said.

" Those days are through." Said Josiah.

Songs of the Black Angels

" Come a little closer." Said Rachael.

" The clouds upon your shoulders." Said Josiah.

" The hope that will lead us to tomorrow." Said Josiah.

" If we hold on." Said Rachael.

" You'll be with us forever." Said Rachael.

" I'm comfortable in God's arms." Said Josiah.

" We will pray for you." Said Rachael.

" Don't worry." Said Rachael.

" His healing comes through mercy." Said Rachael.

" What if I was always here." Said Josiah.

" Would you doubt, through words.
Not enough." Said Rachael.

" We know God is near." Said Josiah.

" You remind us you are near." Said Josiah.

" Your healing comes through your mercy."

" The revealing of this life, the rains, mercy
In your eyes." Said Josiah.

" I was left drowning." Said Josiah.

" To be someone." Said Josiah.

" God is the end and the beginning." Said Rachael.

" God is rising." Said Josiah.

" Listen to the sound." Said Josiah.

" Your mercy flows God." Said Rachael.

" Turn the stereo up." Said Josiah.

" Ceramic unicorns are at your feet." Said Rachael.

" We worship you." Said Josiah.

" Bill Board Magazine." Said Rachael.

" Professionals." Said Josiah.

" Worshiping God is good." Said Josiah.

" The Songs of the Black Angels."

Songs of the Black Angels

" The Songs of the Black Angels
Are worship songs." Said Josiah.
" Wondering if you could ever be loved." Said Rachael.
" You're beautiful.
You're beautiful." Said Josiah.
" The shadow of the cross." Said Josiah.
" Hangs over us." Said Rachael.
" You were meant for
More than this." Said Josiah.
" You are blessed." Said Josiah.
" Ceramic unicorns are at your feet." Said Rachael.
" Heaven is your thrown, earth is your footstool."
Said Josiah.
" These lyrics flow." Said Rachael.
" For someone to notice me four times." Said Rachael.
" You weren't around." Said Josiah.
" Rastafari." Said Josiah.
" Going to wrap it all around." Said Rachael.
" This is good- White Crystal Entertainment." Said Josiah.
" Turn up the stereo." Said Josiah.
" My life is gold." Said Rachael.
" All we need is God's love." Said Rachael.
" I will follow you." Said Josiah.
" I will live for you." Said Josiah.
" Jah love." Said Josiah.
" Jah love." Said Josiah.
" Light up the darkness." Said Rachael.

Songs of the Black Angels

" God is with us." Rachael said.

" Chasing the stars I see you." Josiah said.

" You were the stars." Josiah said.

" Your great name endures." Said Rachael.

" Every fear has no place." Said Josiah.

" Oceans bow to your greatness." Said Rachael.

" Jesus was the Lamb that was slain." Said Josiah.

" Worthy is the Lamb." Said Josiah.

" All the world will praise your name." Said Rachael.

" There are horses of ceramic that bow
At your feet Oh God." Said Rachael.

" Praise your name." Said Josiah.

" Cobras are entwined." Said Rachael.

" Worthy is the Lamb." Said Josiah.

" Worthy is the Lamb that was slain." Said Josiah.

" Jesus is the Lamb that was slain." Said Rachael.

" I don't want to live like I don't care." Said Josiah.

" If I could choose." Said Josiah.

" It's time for me to follow through,
And live the way it was meant for me to." Josiah said.

" The unicorns are white, if I could choose." Said Rachael.

" Winged unicorns bow at your feet Oh God." Said Rachael.

" I have fallen in love with you, and I
Think about you all the time." Said Josiah.

" The emerald unicorns come to you." Said Josiah.

" God's love endures, through all creation." Said Rachael.

" God's love remains." Said Rachael.

" What does it take to make you learn." Said Josiah.

" That God's love endures forever." Said Josiah.

" The prose won't go away." Said Rachael.

" God's love endures." Said Josiah.

Songs of the Black Angels

" Stars of diamond light shine." Said Rachael.

" Upon God." Said Josiah.

" You are the only one for me." Said Rachael

" You are the only one for me." Said Rachael

" Quasars and galaxies shine on you God." Said Josiah.

" Diamonds glow in the dark." Said Josiah.

" This painted universe shines on." Said Josiah.

" You have always been there for me." Said Rachael.

" There are white unicorns in the black galaxy." Said Josiah.

" God you are the only one for me.." Said Rachael.

" Crowns the sun shines on you." Said Josiah.

" As black as it could be. The trinity glows." Said Rachael.

" God took the nails for me, in the light." Said Rachael.

" Rising, your glory is in this place." Said Josiah.

" God you love me, judged me innocent." Said Josiah.

" You rose from the grave." Said Rachael.

" Dying you loved me." Said Josiah.

" You rolled the stone away." Said Josiah.

" Jesus the Lamb that was slain." Said Rachael.

" The storms wash away." Said Josiah.

" You loved us in a broken place." Said Rachael.

" And you mercy shines like the sun." Said Josiah.

" Jesus is the savior of the world." Said Josiah.

" Jesus was the Lamb that was slain." Said Rachael.

" My savior lives." Said Josiah.

Solo. These are songs of the Black Angels.

For we are always praising God in our spirits.

And we live for God.

I think of how you love me.

Beyond the crimson seas.

Where crimson gold shines.

Your light shines on.

Your light shines on.

You are always there for me.

Beyond the rising of the sun and the grave danger.

You light the way as a friend.

You are the light and the way.

You are always there for me.

You shine times four.

You mean everything to me.

Songs of the Black Angels

You sacrifice yourself for me
You are the sails set adrift on the ocean
Always show me the way
You sacrifice yourself for me
I live for you
Show me the power child times two
Unicorns light the way
" As waterfalls run wild." Said Rachael.
" This is your land." Said Josiah.
" You are with us." Said Rachael
" Where there are divisions, tear them down
Oh God." Said Rachael.
" You are the light." Said Josiah.
" That shines." Said Josiah.
The Holy Trinity is with us.
" You are always there for me." Said Josiah.
" He will bring us back to him." Said Rachael.
" Hungry for love." Said Rachael.
" Jah will carry us." Said Josiah.
" But this is how the song goes." Said Josiah.
" This is how it sounds." Said Josiah.

Songs of the Black Angels

Gold ran in our veins.
We lived on Bourbon Street.
For so long I tried to make it to
The top. Rachael and I were doing
Well. But still I tried to make something
Out of my compositions.
The world was like unicorns and
Waterfalls. Beautiful.
        The gold sun shone through
A night with clouds. There were
Blue skies in the night.
For the sky was like gold.
The crescent moon shown.
" I will always love you," said Josiah.
" I will always love you," said Rachael.
" The gold sun shines through the clouds."
Said Josiah.
" And the horizon is stolen." Said Rachael.
" Midnight gold." Said Josiah.
" The angels with white wings
Are all around us." Said Rachael.
" I will always love you." Said Josiah.
" I will always love you." Said Josiah.
There was an angel of David with white wings.
" I will always love you." Said Josiah.
Crosses of silver shown in Rachael's eyes.
The earth shown in Josiah's eyes.
The mansion was old and quiet.
And elegant.
" Rastafari." Said Josiah.

Songs of the Black Angels

" Rastafari." Said Rachael.
There were Niyabinghi drums
In the mansion.
" The sun sets in your eyes."
Said Josiah.
The rain fell from the sky.
" I will always love you." Said Josiah.
Rain fell from the gold sky.
" There are doves that fly." Said Rachael.
" I will always love you." Said Josiah.
" The sky is gold and blue." Said Rachael.
" Doves fly in the night sky." Said Josiah.
The moon was white with an amber
Glow.
Orange dolphins swam in the ocean.
" Do you want some wine." Josiah said.
" You have to talk to Roxane." Said Rachael.
" Roxane is my music manager." Said Josiah.
" Why do I have to speak to her?" Said Josiah.
Angels played on burning violins.
The Cobras rose. The light shown.
" Because you have to progress." Said Rachael.
" Take your music and progress. Said Rachael.
" It's important." Said Rachael.
" Progressive music." Said Josiah.
" Is a larger part of life." Said Josiah.
The Cobras were alive.
Eagles flew through the sky.

Songs of the Black Angels

There were eagles and crows in
The night sky.
" Where's the weed." Said Josiah.
" Shots of Jim Beam." Said Rachael.
The crows flew throughout the sky.
" This is the spirit world." Said Josiah.
The moon looked like an ocean.
Hearts on fire.
The ocean moved to the motion
Of the tides.
Like it was alive.
The hustle and bustle.
Where cities never sleep.
And the lights glowed in the dark.
There were urchins in the water.
Houses in a pink sky at night.
Chariots of fire.
The golden unicorns danced.
" We need to have the tiger's spirit." Said Josiah.
Silhouettes in the moon light.
" We are on fire." Said Josiah.
" Fast to sleep soon to wake and dream." Said Josiah.
Her long fluid motions.
Strong desire.
" How could Haile Selassie be
The second coming of Christ? And
Why does this depict if you're
Rasta or not." Said Rachael.
" Being Rasta is being true
To the good," said Josiah.
" Organized religions aren't the
Path they just point the way." Josiah said.

Songs of the Black Angels

" Rastafari." Said Josiah.
" Heaven isn't too far away. We
Should be mindful. Some people
Go to heaven and some people
Go to hell." Said Rachael.
" Well, I guess not everyone goes
To heaven." Said Rachael.
There was passion in their souls.
Like Christ the lover of souls.
We are redeemed through Christ.
" I guess not." Said Josiah.
" God loves us." Said Josiah.
His eyes showed like midnight.
" Jah lives." Said Rachael.
" Rainbows and butterflies." Said Rachael.
The ceramic unicorns dances.
" It's about New Zion." Said Josiah.
" This is true." Said Josiah.
Golden Unicorns danced in oblivion.
The world was red jade.
Gothic and Gothic cathedrals.
" God is the setting sun." Said Josiah.
" The world is cruel." Said Rachael.
" It can be a cruel place to live." Said Josiah.
The cathedrals towered on the horizon.
" Jah loves the children." Said Rachael.
" He is a lover of souls." Said Josiah.
Tigers crept in the depth of night.
" Redeemer of the world." Said Josiah.
Dragons flew in the depths of night.
There were blue dragons.
Elephants.
Sand fell in an hour glass.

Songs of the Black Angels

Golden Unicorns.
I had dated other
Women in my dating days.
And many of them I fell in
Love with. But Rachael was
Different. She was beautiful.
She was like red jade. Spinning.
We were super heroes and that's
What we were. Not ordinary.
Gold ran in our veins.
I would make it to the top.
In a whirl wind. I was a storm.
PANDA
The gates were iron outside.
The Golden Unicorn Chinese
Restaurant was outside. The world
Was a crystal. Fit for poetry.
RED WHITE AND BLUE
America will survive.
            There is a road to heaven.
There is a highway to hell.
There are angels and there are
Demons. Satan can appear
As an angel of light.
The Cross is what matters.
God's love.
White clouds blew in the wind.
The night was quiet.
SAINTS
MORPHINE
The world spun and I was
Shattered like a vase.
Graffiti
STEELERS
Liquid. Diamonds shine in the light.
The amber roses weep.

Songs of the Black Angels

Heart of trance.
Bass.
Trance rhythms of violet.
Roses burn in the waking hours.
Daffodils.
" You loved me through the
Winter of my soul." Said Josiah.
" Thanks a lot." Said Rachael Ray.
Owls flew on desolate waters.
DAFFODILS
Jesus is the morning glory.
Jesus has a morning glory sword.
The Lord carries us.
God is perpetual light.
The light shines on and on.
Red sky. This is my heart.
The heart that was broken.
INRI
Skull Hill live forever.
Angels are all around.
Slay the dragon. Blue dragons. Gold dragons.
The gold dragons are by the river.
There is a river of love.
Down.
Bourbon Street. Blue skulls.
The gold dragons drink by the river.
The light in on at the restaurant
Golden Unicorn.
Love brings me down.
The blue dragons drink by the river.
Down
Peach Schnapps. Sun set.

Songs of the Black Angels

Jesus loves us.
There's only one messiah.
Rain washes down.
Doves cry in love.
" You're either Rasta or you're
not."
" Organized religion sucks."
" Rastafari ever living."
" You are beautiful Rachael," I said.
" You are beautiful too," said Rachael.
DIEZ
" I want to spend the rest of my life with
you." Said Josiah.
" I want to spend the rest of my life with
you." Said Rachael.
" I wish these times lasted forever." Said Rachael.
" So do I." Said Josiah.
The sun set at night.
Mercury could be seen in the sky.
" I thirst under these quiet skies," said Josiah.
Oceans were blue.
Mercury
" So many people try to be Rasta,
But they're not because they don't
Live according to the natural world."
Said Rachael.
" Jesus was flesh and blood."
" Rasta is upholding the natural world."
Said Josiah.
" There's little talk about buds." Josiah said.
" It's taboo like other things." Said Rachael.
" But there is a revolution going on." Said Josiah.
" People have to be educated." Said Rachael.
" Straight edge is in."

Songs of the Black Angels

Violets and blue.
" Our religion is Christianity and
Will survive." Said Josiah.
" We survive." Said Rachael.
King Diamond
" What is the lost story." Said Josiah.
" Kryptonite." Said Rachael.
" Where do they keep the real doctors at."
Said Josiah.
" The seed is the highest form." Said Josiah.
" Rastas come together to celebrate
Life." Said Rachael.
" Treating women unfairly is
Not hip." Said Josiah.
" Women don't have less rights."
Said Rachael.
" Reggae is a pure art form." Said Josiah.
" It's unlike the manmade world. Babylon."
Said Josiah.
Jokers are wild.
" Nothing beats the Kings card not
Even an ace." Said Josiah.
" The Ace of Spades." Said Rachael.
" There was music playing at a
Carnival outside. This is in 54."
Said Josiah.
" Not four four." Said Josiah.

Songs of the Black Angels

" Freedom of speech everyone else
Got to write what they want." Said Josiah.
FREEDOM BEING
" When is the world going to evolve."
Said Josiah.
" The world is an enemy in the
Christian faith." Said Rachael.
" That and the Devil, the
Powers of hell." Said Rachael.
Inez
Vinoodh Matadin
Forever
" The Bible says we became an enemy
To God." Said Josiah.
" The Bible is the book of life."
Said Rachael.
" The enemy is the world,
The Devil and the powers of hell."
Said Josiah.
" Reggae is music of the art." Said Josiah.
" Jah lives." Said Rachael.
" No one claims to be God in the
Flesh, only Jesus did." Said Josiah.
PURPLE DOVES
Blue People
" Crying Buddha is a good band."
Said Rachael.

Songs of the Black Angels

" They're divine." Said Rachael.
" They're composed of nine black
Angles and a star. And they are
Prayer warriors. Dragons." Said
Rachael.
" We fight to survive," said Josiah.
" The world spins along it's axis."
Said Rachael.
Rattlesnakes
" We live in a world governed
By angels." Said Josiah.
" Angels." Said Josiah.
" And filled with saints." Said Rachael.
" We're close to the kingdom of heaven."
Said Josiah.
Black Cobras
" We live in a world of Painted Dragons.
Prayer warriors and criminals." Said Josiah.
" Jesus was flesh and blood." Said Rachael.
" God's grace is with us." Said Josiah.
" We are like the angels." Said Rachael.
" This sonic creation." Said Josiah.
Digital
" The world of cameras and enlightenment."
Said Josiah.
" Planet earth rages." Said Rachael.
FAITH
" Draw near to the white light." Said Josiah.
" Jah loves us." Said Rachael.
" We're like Indians." Said Josiah.
" But not from India." Said Josiah.
" You should have told me." Said Rachael.
" You would be there for me." Said Rachael.
" Sometimes all we can do is hold
On." Said Rachael.
" I love you." Said Josiah.

Songs of the Black Angels

Blue dragons flew in an infinite sky.
People say creeds.
There are cherubs around us.
" I love you like 14 carat gold."
Said Josiah.
" This dream play out." Said Rachael.
God is great.
" We hold the keys to our hearts."
Said Josiah.
" Possessive." Josiah said.
Rachael began laughing.
Prayers
" Prayer warriors are important to
The body of Christ." Said Josiah.
" I could hold you in my arms
Forever." Said Josiah.
Prayer warriors are called dragons.
Take my hand.
Hope extinguished by light.
We hold on.
" God so love the world that
He gave his only son that
Whosoever believes in him
Should not perish but have
Everlasting life."
Life

Songs of the Black Angels

Everlasting life.
" It's time to take a step of
Faith."
" His one and only son."
" At the cross we're saved."
Obsession.
" Singers that cry are beautiful."
Said Josiah.
" Our breathing heart poets
And artists." Said Rachael.
Statues stand in the rain.
The stones look like angels.
Jack Daniels.
House.
Kile Wang
White voice.
Poles
" Rastafari." Said Rachael.
" Women's right."
Rain washes away the pain.
Blood and desire.
New York City
It's gripping, the pain." Said Rachael.
White Rum
The streets will build us up.
Communication.
War-torn.
Iron Curtain
New York, New York
Desire
" Love is what hold us." Said Rachael.
" I love you Mercedes." Said Josiah.
That was my girl Mercedes.
We talked until the dawns.
Night passed.

Songs of the Black Angels

I was having a long conversation
With Rachael and I thought it was
Appropriate. Being that we
Loved each other.
Love is all we need.
We were in the Mansion and
There were angels of stone in the
Rain. Angels of stone.
Their wings unbound all
But gold. We were the chosen
Ones. A chosen race. Just as God
Has children so does Jesus. The gates
Were like the gates of heaven.
Heaven. Heaven is greater than
English. I prefer the vernacular.
Otherwise just cultural biases.
What words were ok to use and
Which ones aren't.
What is ok to say and what
Isn't. " Are you saved?"
Is something you say to the
Next one?
And if so how does that make
You feel.
There are hopes and
Hopes to be challenged.

Songs of the Black Angels

Spring. Spring is a season
Of newborn life. Hope.
Only hope. Hopes.
We are who we are.
The angels were like
Stone in the rain.
Strong arms of hope, dignity,
Honor. Not passive aggression.
The angels were like stone. I
Watched them outside the window
In the night.
Clutches. Grasps. We're in the angels
Clutches. Softly. Night is like a
Stranger. Sometimes the nights
Are hard. Life is not easy.
Neither is breaking bread.
The angles were all around.
I watched the rain fall.
Angels are all around.
Life goes by.
" We're Rastafarians," said Rachael.
" But we're not into the organized religion
Of it we're not into organized religion
At all." Said Rachael.
What's better is to know the
Angels are all around.

Songs of the Black Angels

The skyscrapers stood on the
Horizon. The mountains stood
Tall. The sun shown at night
Like an eclipse of the sun.
God's grace is with us.
God's mercy endures forever.
The yellow sun shown.
Nights were gold.
I finally had what I desired for
And that was Rachael.
I finally didn't have to live
With the desire. Everything
Became perfect in a moment of
Time. Rachael laughed in the
Night.
The sky was cloudy.
New York
Los Angeles
I will drink the rain.
We'd wash away with the rain.
MIC MALTZAN
" Who ever said love wasn't
Meant to be." Said Rachael.
English is an imposed colonial language.
" Our love is forever ." Said Josiah.
I am a crystal shattered.
" Our love is forever." Josiah said
" Our love is forever." Josiah said.
Just say no to Babylon.
" Black angels are like black doves." Said Rachael.
We'd wash away with the rain.
" If pain would ever leave me alone." Said Rachael.
We'd wash away with the rain.
MALTZAN
We'd wash away with the rain.
As the rain falls.
And the pain remains.
We'd wash away with the rain.

Songs of the Black Angels

When the pain remains.
Can you feel the thunder.
Can we make a new heaven for
You and I.
Because you've been around
And the pain remains
Like silk in the cold night.
The violet withers.

Rain falls on a stone cross.
Outside my window the rain falls.
The rain falls on the stone angels.
The pain will wash away.
The daffodils and the roses stay.
We hold the pain.
And the violet rain falls.
Could there be a new heaven for
Us to be in love.
The old heaven stolen from
Our touch.
The shadows fleet in the sun.
Love is forever.
Black
Could I be myself as the rain
Falls on doves. Doves in
Flight in the sunlight.
God's promise is the rainbow.
The storms are blue.
Violet
Orange violet are the shores

Songs of the Black Angels

I will make my way.
Under this sky
This Milky Way.
The universe stretches on.
The beautiful sun on me
And the precious snow melt streams.
Saints
Blood, beating heart.
Hearts entwined. Heaven's
Shores. The silence of the lambs.
Where angels roam.
The forgotten road.
We're in the hands
Of the angels.
That carry us home.
The forever shores where
Lambs roam and all is silent.
We'll wash away with the rain.
Flowers wash away.
The stars shine in the quiet nights.
Steel breeze
Oblivion
Eternity
FOREVER
" I'll be loving Jah fovever."
Said Rachael.
" We'll be loving Jah forever."
Said Josiah.
Rainbows
Rainbows and Saints
Saints and Angels
Bible Mathew

Songs of the Black Angels

Bible
Baptists
" We'll be forever loving Jah."
Said Josiah.
London
Church of Christ
Church
The Lord carries us.
There are demons and angels.
We cling to angels.
SAINTS
WHITE
Stone angels won't wash away with
The rain.
.SBPRA

Jah Rastafari

" Jah is Emperor." Said Josiah.
" Rastafari arose in the Christian
Culture." Said Josiah.
" We should reject the things
That have to do with Babylon."
Said Rachael.
" Reggae is its own language."
Said Josiah.
" Reggae is its own language."
Said Rachael.
" Down Babylon." Said Josiah.
" Down in the trenches Babylon."
Said Rachael.

Songs of the Black Angels

Irie
Ites
" Our Idren are ours alone." Said Rachael.
" We don't give up to Babylon." Said Josiah.
" Babylon is fallen." Said Rachael.
" We love each one." Said Josiah.
IRIE
White light
" Jah Rastafari is God." Said Josiah.
White Dove
" You're either Rasta or you believe
Something else. Something sacred." Said Rachael.
" That which is sacred should be
Kept sacred." Said Rachael.
" That which is ours is ours
To keep." Said Rachael.
" Love is a bleeding rose." Said Josiah.
" And the cool hours pass." Said Josiah.
" What is there than that which we love."
Said Rachael.
Love of the blue skies.
Love of the blue skies.
I finally got what I wanted and that
Was Rachael Ray.
The hours passed and we talked.
" If we can hold on to what
We have. And never let go."
Said Josiah.
" Love is a bleeding rose." Said Josiah.
" The roses are scarlet and are like the
Nights that pass before our eyes." Said Josiah.

Songs of the Black Angels

" Have you ever loved someone and
Felt that you were drowning in
A sea of roses?" Said Josiah.
" Talk, you can say whatever
You want to say." Said Rachael.
" Violets fall in seas of illusion.
Love is the basis for everything."
Said Josiah.
" I don't want to let go. I don't
Want death to separate us." Said Josiah.
" Neither do I," Said Rachael.
" I don't want anything to separate us."
Said Rachael.
" Love is the only thing we have. Love
Conquers all in illusions." Said Rachael.
" But why did I have to say goodbye
To those I loved. It makes me lose
Faith." Said Josiah.
" Friends are not around
Forever is what I supposed
To say, but I'm not going to.
There are paths in life. And not
Always are we on the same path."
Said Rachael.
" You've lost people I understand
That because they went their
Separate ways. And no one can prepare
Themselves for losing friends. It's
A real thing. And the pain is real."
Said Rachael.
" I miss Whitney." Josiah started
To cry.
" You're not working." Said Rachael

Songs of the Black Angels

" I haven't seen Whitney." Said Josiah
As he cried.
" Whitney is ok though. You guys
Are like brothers." Said Rachael.
" Time heals wounds you weren't
Meant to be separated from Whitney.
You're old friends you just have some
Catching up to do."
" Do you think it would be alright."
Said Josiah.
" It will be fine." Said Rachael.
" But I have a heart too.
And I feel you. You're vibing with me
And you know you're right there."
Said Rachael.
" Look at the night sky." Said Rachael.
" We deserve to be together." Said Rachael.
" The night sky is blue." Said Rachael.
Her blue eyes shown through the
Night.
Spider 6 flew through the air.
Mars shown through the sky.
"Positive vibrations." Said Rachael.
" Whitney is my brother in Christ.
I don't want to be apart." Said Josiah.
Rachael said, " Just vibe it's everlasting love."
Rachael said, " You can pour your heart
Onto paper with your lyrics but you
Have to take things in stride. Record
Companies are not going to change
Over night."
Rachael said, " Stay on top. Be a wild fire
But don't burn out Josiah. Too many of
The greats burned out we don't need
Any more loss."
Rachael said, " You're the greatest singer
In the world. The world doesn't know

Songs of the Black Angels

Superheroes first hand. They know us
Our common identities. You've been
Able to succeed and that's great."
" The thing about the singer Scott
Stevens is he was a great singer
But he died from an overdose.
He didn't keep a cool head. You
Have to keep a cool head." Said Rachael.
We wash away.
" People are sensitive." Said Rachael.
" But the music world has lost people
Do to drugs and overdose, and it's
Truly devastating." Said Rachael.
" Our strength comes from Christ." Said Rachael.
" The world is like a crystal." Said Rachael.
" We only see what we want to see
And looks can be deceiving." Said Rachael.
" It's not the Father's heart that even one
Should perish." Said Rachael.
Josiah and Rachael were Rastas.
There were old pictures of Buddhist monks
Around the living room of the mansion from
Searching. They were old pictures.
" Love is a bleeding rose." Said Rachael.
" Josiah when we first met I knew
You were the one. I stayed with that
Because my blood flows.

Lilly

Songs of the Black Angels

You're the best singer in the world
Prayer warriors need to pray too. We
Need prayer from the enemy." Said
Rachael.
The moon spun.
Oceans of love.
Day after day.
And I slowly feel the pain.
I hear her voice
Lingering, but nothing could stop my mind.
We should live forever.
And life is a common
Diamond. In which we're all a part.
" I'll always be with you." Said Rachael Ray.
It was a world of super heroes.
The moon was black on the horizon.
Blue skies at night.
Josiah looked into Rachael's eyes.
There were two young lovers.
" We have to wait for the crimson
Moon." Was Rachael's way of
Saying we have to wait until the
Time is right. Timing.
The golden sky was overhead.
We should live forever.

Lilly

Songs of the Black Angels

Lyrics Where ever you go I
Will play the game to remain
in love with you.
Life is a violet rose.
Saint Michael slay the serpent.
There are angels
Waiting for you.
Whatever you see
I want to see it too.
I want to spend the time with you.
Oceans flow.
I slowly feel the pain
Of having to love it all.
When I'm a broken crystal.
I will carry you.
The moon will be waiting for you.
I see her laughter
I slowly feel the pain.
But the pain doesn't stop the years.
Love sees it our way.
Love the bleeding rose.
The rose sun grows cold.
I think we should be together.
I will be there for you.
I slowly feel the pain.
I don't have the time.
Sand falls through my hands.
To heal all my wounds
Until I make love whole
I am on this island alone.

Lilly

Songs of the Black Angels

And I cannot stop the time.
" I am on an island of flowers."
Said Josiah.
" I see it your way. Love
Is faithful to
The end and there is no end just
New beginnings." Said Rachael.
We had been betrayed.
Lyrics The rain falls
And crimson violets float down
This is glamorous
The beauty and the pain
I wish it all away
Down Down
The sunset falls
And the crimson sun flows
Down the river and the sea
Flow down
The lights ignite the flame
Down
Deceit. The sea. Flowers float down.
" Rastas should be who they are
Not what organized religion makes
Them out to be." Said Josiah.
" The sun sets pink." Said Rachael.
Black angels are born.
Deceit runs down.
The night is cold.
The world is ice.
Crystal clear.
Straight edge.
" Why then am I accused of doing
Drugs." Said Josiah.
" I'm supposed to
Support them? Said Josiah.

Lilly

Songs of the Black Angels

" No Josiah everyone is judged
At some point or another. You have
To be who you are not what others
Make you out to be." Said Rachael.
" The world is black stone." Said Josiah.
Lyrics The river runs down
We drag ourselves down
I thought today was about love
You made it about other things
When we find the way
Love will find the way
Love will keep us alive
The flowers are prayers
For us to share
As the flowers fall down
The river and the sea run down
The ocean breeze flows down
" We'll stay alive."
My white painted face.
The black paint and the grave.
How long we've been alive.
There are beautiful people around
Us. They hold us up as angels fall
Down.
Angels fall and float down.
There are loving people around us.
" You're Rasta if you love one another
And believe in natural things." Said Josiah.
" Love will keep us alive." Said Rachael.

Songs of the Black Angels

This black lace dream.
Seas of lies.
What keeps us alive?
The motion of our steps is
Down.
Flowers and the sand fall
Down.
" Haile Selassie is part
Of speech is part of language."
Said Josiah.
" Haile Selassie was a world
Leader." Said Josiah.
Doves cry at night.
Doves fly under the rainbows.
What is ours is
What keeps us alive.
" Look at the night sky." Said Rachael.
" Love is faithful to the end." Said Rachael.
" Love is what keeps us alive." Said Rachael.
" Rastafari is not a religion it's a culture.:
" Vibe." Said Josiah.
" Positive Vibrations." Said Josiah.
" Rastafari." Said Josiah.
" We shouldn't put trends above
God. Nor current trends. We have
To stay with the Father.
The Father loves us." Said Josiah.
" We are in the Father's arms." Said
Josiah. The crows were like rainbows
 outside. There was thunder.

Songs of the Black Angels

Merit
Ga Ga

The world was grey. Broken dreams. What was there but broken
dreams. I'm only going to break your heart. We belong to Zion. Fire.
Earth   Fire   Water

Honor
Respect
Love

There is such thing as human kind. There is such thing as love.
Love Conquers All
I was religious. And I was a Christian. I believed Jesus was the
Son of God. Rastafari was not a better religion. But I believed in the
medicinal use of marijuana. I just didn't know a lot about the plant. The
use of the plant would depend on studies. Everyone is entitled to their
beliefs. Good can come from anything. Nor did I believe that females
were less important.
    These things were obvious. What was the use in trying when all I
could do was break your heart. I have dreadlocks like Rachael. I was
against Babylon, but not human beings and certainly not.
    There was no way out. The only direction was down. What good
could come from trying? The river and the sun go down.
    I was sweating this girl. I always had money on my mind. Life was
a delicate flower. Let's face it constitutions are meaningless. Love is
tragic. Sometimes in a river of deceit. What good could come? Shattered
like a crystal. Down.
    Thank God our souls go to heaven. The river of the soul goes down.
The only direction is down.
    Crossbones
Hope of the white light.
Love
Dignity
Honor
    The river of the soul goes down. The stars in the midnight sky go
down. Everything is black. The only direction is down. The white rose

falls down. The world is ruin. The stars in the sky go down. Hallelujah glory.

Our souls go down. Heaven is to be found. Hearts unbound. The direction of love is down. The white rose falls down. Look at me now.

Songs of the Black Angels

You don't understand you thought I was so close to her. Look at me now this decorated life could bring. Her hands go down.

The direction of the stars is down. What could life be. You don't have to treat me this way. The white souls go down. The river of your soul goes down. The only direction is down.
Crystal flowers in a tube. Flowers fall down. Doves of pearl go down. The world was a hole.

Lyrics Black sun
Starlight shine on me
Wash away the pain
I have waited for the day
When I could see her
The years have gone down
And I wait for her
What are we doing
This for if it's not for love
Our souls are like tulips
It hurts to be held
To feel the warmth of love
I wish I said things differently
I should have told you
How I felt before it was too late

The years had gone by. They were precious years, years I have spent with Rachael Ray. The world was stolen. It wasn't new. Like I mentioned earlier Rachael and I were inseparable.

Skull and Crossbones
We were fearless.
" Rachael where does the time go?" Said Josiah.
" I don't know." Said Rachael.

I thought about Viper. I hadn't kept in touch with my friends since I have started dating Rachael seriously. The years had gone by.

The rainbow was God's promise in the sky.

Who ever said falling in love was easy.

Black angels fly above oceans.

Flowers fall through a dark sky. It is hard to describe what life was like knowing that I was going to lose something. But I had Rachael's hand. It was only me.

" So have you spoken to Lucidia." Asked Rachael. " No I haven't gone to see the oracle. She told me last time that I wouldn't have to be coming back. She said something about a fire." Said Josiah. " How it would burn." Said Josiah. " What did you just say?" Said Rachael. " The oracle said something about a fire." Josiah repeated.

Rachael said, " That's me." " The oracle was talk about me." Josiah laughed. Rachael was possessive. A diamond of promise. " Being Rastafarian is cultural." Said Josiah.

" But what about the past." Rachael said.

" Rachael I don't know how many times we have had this conversation." Said Josiah.

Songs of the Black Angels

" You can't, it's against me that I dated before you." Said Josiah." I don't hold it against you. I'm so sure." Rachael then laughed.

" Well what about them?" Said Rachael. " Well I wanted to marry Anhia. She was my first love." Said Josiah. " That was when you lived at home still. I don't even want to have this conversation." Said Rachael.

" Well everyone grows up." Said Josiah. " Yeah but you didn't have to." Said Rachael. Josiah started to laugh.

" Well I broke up with Anhia and Venessa and they were both serious relationships." " I know I'm only kidding you. You didn't even know me yet." Said Rachael.

" I'll never forget how we met. It was after you broke up with Vanessa. Yeah I remember that." Said Rachael.

" Well I thought I was going to marry Anhia but the relationship didn't work out." Said Josiah.

Van Heusen

" Yeah your forgetting that the girls you dated were bitches." Said Rachael. " I know that. It's just they were people and I loved them." Said Josiah.

" Of course you did." Said Rachael. " There's nothing wrong with loving people. You did nothing wrong I'm just jealous." Said Rachael.

" Well I should be thankful for what I have. And that is you." Said Josiah. " We are going to live a happy life." Said Rachael. " But we are super heroes." Said Rachael. " We're not like other people." Said Rachael. " But we can live as people and we should be thankful for this." Said Rachael.

" I agree." Said Josiah.

Songs of the Black Angels

" Who we are and who we are in
Our day jobs means a lot. You're
Josiah Young and you're Eagle Hawk.
I'm Rachael Ray. Ice." Said Rachael.
" And yet we're Rastas." Said Josiah.
" I came out of art school. Where
Everyone is strange. People with
Purple and green hair. People
Taking their snakes to school
With them." Said Josiah.
" I'm kinda glad I'm a super hero.
I don't have to follow the world."
Said Josiah. " You are Eagle
Hawk. I'm Ice.
Eagle Hawk had a premonition and
Saw through the eyes of a Hawk.
Ice felt the cold. But that cold that
I felt was from the world. It is a
Cold place to live." Said Rachael
Ray.
        " We have to help
Humanity," Said Rachael.
" Well you dated before you met
Me. I didn't date before I met you.
And you dated a lot of people."
Said Rachael. "Yeah, that's true
I dated a lot of people." Said
Josiah. " I know about them, I
Practically have them memorized."
Said Rachael.
" What were you like in college?"
Said Rachael. " Well I had a
Tough time in college because
My counselor told me that my
Mother was a psychopath."
Said Josiah.

Songs of the Black Angels

" But you can live in real freedom
Here in the United States. Think
About how much freedom you
Have. Think about how much
Freedom you have in New
York City." Said Rachael.
" That has to do with bad shit."
Said Rachael. " It would have
Taken me 100 years to figure
That out." Said Rachael.
Mount Carmel
PROSPECT
" Your counselor told you that?"
Said Rachael.

Paper Supply

" She told you that so you didn't
 Have subliminal shit going on
Josiah that's bad shit."
" I know I was having a hard time
Sleeping and so on." Said Josiah.
" Good counseling will do that."
Said Rachael.
" That was with Christine Diablo.
She is one of us." Said Rachael.
" Josiah we have one another.
While a world revolution goes
On it's better for us to stay in.
We'll go out again later. Give it
Some time." Said Rachael.
" Babylon is against Jah's
Children. We should be thankful
And praise Jah." Said Josiah.
" The world is like Babylon. That's

Songs of the Black Angels

Why we call it that. Babylon from
The Bible. Babylon was bad. The
World is an enemy to Christians.
The world is an enemy to Rastas.
Rastas have a religious preference."
Said Josiah. " Well forget the
Chinese Mafia." Said Rachael.
" What I want to know about is
Vanessa." Said Rachael.
INTERNAL GUNG FU
" Vanessa and I dated for eight months.
Alright Rachael. But I wasn't supposed
To be with her you know." Said
Josiah. " You know." Said Rachael
As she poked fun. " The maroon
Sun shines on." Said Josiah, meaning
You have to move on in life.
" Little Miss Ray, how are you."
Said Josiah.
" I'm well but you think that
You're getting out of talking
About Vanessa and you're
Not. We're talking about her."
Said Rachael.
" I want to know like everything.
I'm not just going to drop it."
Said Rachael. Her jealousy was just.
" Well I met Vanessa after I moved
Out to Cedar Fields. She asked
Me out on a date and we drove
To the clouds in the mountains."
Said Josiah. Everyone has a past."
Said Rachael.

Songs of the Black Angels

" There were jewels around her.
I made Vanessa an angel. But
She wasn't." Said Josiah.
" Ooh I want to get her." Said
Rachael.
" Vanessa betrayed me. She
Hooked up with her ex-boyfriend
And then defended him and them
To my face." Said Josiah.
" Why did she say that she loved
Kevin? She makes no sense. And
She could have told you that they
Were lovers she lied from the
Beginning and there was no point
In her cheating on you." Said Rachael.
" I want to be called Angelica because
You treat me like an angel. You treat
Me like a princess, and I'm happy with
The way you treat me." Said Rachael.
" But why did he come out to see her
In the first place. I thought they were
Broken up."
" They were she even said that she
Didn't like him." Said Josiah.
" Then why did she cheat on you.
You did nothing to deserve that. She
Got back with her ex-boyfriend and
Then lied about it. What were you
Supposed to do?" Said Rachael.

Songs of the Black Angels

SOUL TO DARE
" I was just yelling at her. I was like
Vanessa are you or are you not
With him. And she said ' I love
Him,'" said Josiah.
" She defended him and
She defended them. She
Defended them." Said Josiah.
DARE TO FLY
BUDDHA
Lyrics How could you walk
    Out of my life
    When all I did
    Was watch you leave
    We shared the pain
    Of loving one another
    And the rain falls down
    And the rain falls down
    I feel the sorrow in my veins
    When all I did was watch
    You breathe
    We dared to walk through
    The pain
    And the rain falls down
    The rain falls down
    The rain falls down

    The rain falls down
    The rain falls down
    The rain falls down

Moon Days T.O.D. THE ECLIPSE

Songs of the Black Angels

" But she never explained why
She would just cheat on you.
Why what explanation does she
Have." Said Rachael.
" I wish it was easier to
Get over. She truly started a
Flame. She just didn't love
Me. And I loved her." Said
Josiah.
" All your relationships were
Stupid." Said Rachael.
Rachael and Josiah laughed.
" Vanessa just went away.
After I called her out and
Told her I knew she was
Cheating on me she went away."
Said Josiah.
Down.

Songs of the Black Angels

" But how can I even have this
Conversation with you they're
Ex's." Said Josiah. Rachael said,
" That's not even the point. You
Weren't doing anything. She is
The one who created the problems
Not you, you did nothing wrong.
What is her deal. The ex's thing is
Not important. That doesn't
Interfere with us. You got me
Fair and square."
Flowers fall down.
Rachael said, " I was walking the
Streets of Harlem when you were
Dating Vanessa. Don't baby me
Just because you were my first
Boyfriend. Vanessa had the
Problem she is the one who did
All those things. She cheated on
You and she had no reason to.
She could have just as easily
Broken up with you. She had no
Reason." Rachael said, " Your
Girlfriends had their own problems,
Whatever, those issues were not you."
" Josiah you're the best singer in
The world, you're forgetting these
Girls are low. And let me tell you
Another thing they are low for
What they did."
" Well people believe what people
Believe. I dated regularly and all
The girls I was meeting were
Cheating on me."
" Yeah but they're the losers, they

Songs of the Black Angels

Lost because they were dumb.
Alright I'm not going to put it like
A poet they were dumb and they
Did dumb shit." Said Rachael.
" What a mouth." Said Josiah.
Rachael began laughing with
Josiah. " Those girls had no right
Treating you like trash. No right."
Josiah laughed.
" And your saying you are judged
For doing drugs. Who are these
People you are a recovering addict.
You made it out alive. I'm sorry these
People bother me they don't know
What's up. Said Rachael.
" Vanessa was the love of your life
She had no right to cheat on you.
I'm sorry but that was completely
Uncalled for. She is still a sista
You don't go and walk all over
Someone." Rachael said.
" I'm sorry but you don't treat
People the way she treated you.
You don't go fucking with peoples
Lives. You don't do that shit."
Said Rachael.
Flowers fall down.
" Well Venessa said they were
Only friends. That's before he
Even came up." Said Josiah.

Songs of the Black Angels

" Yeah you know what all those
 Girls you dated had problems.
You know why they're not
Super heroes. That's why."
Josiah and Rachael laughed.
" People dancing on you
Is not sacred I'm sorry." Said Rachael.
" Well Ahnia was the beginning.
Venessa was just as hard to break
Up with." Said Josiah.
" You should have been touring
Those girls aren't squat. They
Don't know what they had. They
Don't know who they are. Said Rachael.
Rachael said, " You met me during
A very beautiful time. But we're
Rastas we know what's up.
Actions are important. I used
To dance to the music I could
Feel the freedoms in my veins.
Those girls were sucky."
" Sucky?" Josiah said and Rachael
And Josiah started laughing.
" They're great sucky great sucky."
Josiah joked.
" The point I'm trying to make is
That they had no business doing
The things they did. They could
Have broken it off you don't drag
Someone into your problems."
Said Rachael.
" You're such a good person. Those
Girls didn't know what's up." Said

Songs of the Black Angels

Rachael. " I'm in a world of my
Own what I create comes from
My studio work. I push myself
In my sessions." Said Josiah.
" You brought me into your
World when you married me.
I made out." " But I'm protective
Of you. Every super hero has
Had a touch go of it in peoples'
World. We're super heroes
We're different." Rachael said.
Route Ten 1515
Empire City
Red Sky
1:06 AM
Blue Night
" We should have been engaged
Longer Josiah." Said Rachael.
" But that's what love is all about."
Said Josiah. The world is a
Beautiful place. Bury me
Softly. I can only
Break your heart. Sand rains
Down and here I am. Holding
Red flowers in a tube. Ignorance
Is bliss some say. But I want it
All. What is love but a battle,
Between good and evil. I hold
Red flowers in a tube. Though
The storms have blown in I know
were still here with me, though
I don't know for how long. Who
Is your friend and who is your
Worst enemy? Who ties all love
In knots. And who clips our
Wings. I want to fly away with
You but I don't know how and

Songs of the Black Angels

I don't know where. Or where
To go for you bring me down.
I wish you were here with me,
Where the flowers bloom, but
You're on the other side where
Chains and broken bottles tell
The story of our unearthly addictions.
I wish I loved you sometimes but
 it's better if you go, and I hold
red flowers in a tube. For you I
would do anything, and I'm torn
in love and hate collide.
You're not what I am looking for.
So it's better if you go and leave
The past behind. Instead of feeding
The fire of our addictions. Your green
Eyes and blonde hair… You were
 All I ever want. When I loved you
I was sane. But this broken glass
That I hold is like your heart and
It would be better if you went home
And never came back. Then I wouldn't
Be holding on to these red flowers.
When the flowers bloom I think of you
And hold on to all I ever wanted, and
That was anything from you. I don't
Love you, I just remember the past.
You can't clip the angels wings to fly.
And what you do you would do to
Angels so it seems.

Song of the Black Angels

In this madness and rhythm of our
Lives. I'll never forget you or the
Way you walked out the door.
I can't love you anymore. You
Broke too many promises which
I held dear. Now you grab at what
You can, and judge me like you do
The angels. For what I don't know.
But I sit and drink this apple juice.
 And I know
I'll live. Bury me softly.
I know your love from afar. You
Lucidly drifted into the bar. Where I
Work and pretend we're still
Together but apart. I never loved
Anything as much as I loved her.
But you take what you can't give
And don't let go. I've seen your
Face before, and the flowers in your
Hair. And I thought love was easy.
But the pain reminds me that nothing
Is so sacred without you. I lost you
When I said hello at the bar. And
You walked into every joint there was
Looking for me. As if I owed you my
Time. But finally after years have past
I can honestly say your mad. And I
Don't belong to you and your crazy

Songs of the Black Angels

Love. I can't own the things you give.
I lay it all down to go on. And I dream
Like I did before you. The black angels
Sing when I'm sad and when your around.
Otherwise it's the white angels. Who cry
In the solemn mornings of gold. They open
Their wings to fly to God and return
To protect me from you. For love is like a
Battle when you're around. And it
Wages on in my soul. I dream of innocence.
And uncharted fear. In the solemn mornings
Of gold. I tear up the words you gave to me
And pour water into the fire. For
How could you just stand there and watch
And not say a word to me. While I mourned
And this goes on in life, but you send
The angels to God. And you break hearts
Like glass. And you are beautiful. How
Deceiving looks can be. How softly I that
dream. Love is the machine. And the battle
the wages onto the night. You were
never there for me.
Lyrics I write but can't face
        The burning desire
        Flowers burn, and paper
        What was there was lost
        And I have paid the cost
        Of love

Songs of the Black Angels

" Trust is a never ending fire." Said
Rachael. The echo of her voice down
Halls. " Let it burn." She said.
Josiah said, " I thought love rare."
" But a poet loves words." Said Rachael.
" The angels fall gracefully." Said
Josiah.
" They fall through the sky." Said
Josiah. " What is there but love."
Said Josiah. " Holding me softly."
Lyrics Roses fall down
       And here I am in the dark
       Night of my soul.
       The sun is black
 " Trust is earned not bought." Said Rachael.
" You love me and that's why I
Fall asleep at night. I can feel that
You're here with me. I just wanted
To talk. To pass the time. There is a
Revolution going on. And we're two
Super heroes that can let things
Work out without crime fighting."
" It not a good time to fight crime."
Said Josiah. " This is fine,
Everything worked out."
" What then do you say we make
A toast." Said Rachael. " A toast so
Shall it be." Said Josiah. " To good
Health." Said Josiah. " To good health."
Said Rachael.

Songs of the Black Angels

Lyrics Gold roses are in bloom
    The clouds are violet and red
    I have these feelings beneath
    I give these words to you
    Though you hardly speak
    The sky cries the words you speak
    There's nothing
    Of this surface deep
    The sky is gold and flowers run
    In the rain that falls under the sun
    The gold roses are in bloom
    I give this part of me to you
    The violet sky is on fire beneath
    We dug our relationship up
    And killed the flowers.
    The violet of the love your lent
    But not a tide you gave to me
    There's nothing
    Of this surface deep
    The sky is gold and flowers run
    In the rain that falls under the sun

    I give this part of me to you

" When you walked into my world I knew
You were meant for me." Said Rachael
" Our marriage is a beautiful memory."
Said Rachael.
" I know that you have always been there
For me. And I'm grateful for that. I don't
Know what I would do without you." Rachael
Began to cry. Two lovers.

Songs of the Black Angels

" It's important to be balanced
In body, mind, soul and spirit.
The spirit-man has to be strong."
Said Josiah.
" Balance is an important element
Of life." Rachael returned.
She was like a rose on the water
Roses surround her
She was everything
Losing my soul
Losing my soul
Losing my soul
Losing my soul

Losing my soul
Losing my soul
Losing my soul
Losing my soul

Waves on the sea
I want to fly
Across the oceans
And the grey sky

The clouds roll by

White lions fly

O'Mary Ozim

Ga Ga

Trance is the music of
The soul. We once
Played under the star
Spackled sky. We
Would play drums for
Hours. We were free then.
Free and in tune with life.
We knew of the higher power.
God the Father. God the Son. God
the Holy Spirit. We were free.

Songs of the Black Angels

Rachael was a wildfire. She was
Intelligent, well-mannered and
Beautiful. I loved her, and she loved
Me. We spent much time talking,
The world was in a revolution.
And love, like songs, went on
Between us. Like gold roses
We tangled and tangled amidst
 thorns. The Thorns of roses
were blue. The blue skies forever.
Love the bleeding rose…
Hearts of steel. The heavy ore
Of a terrible machine called
Love… Bleeding roses. Machines
Beat with steel. The steel breeze
Was cool. I was a wealthy
Singer, but I wanted to be a
Writer. I decided to take a
Hiatus and go into writing.
Rachael was everything to
Me. We held each other
During the dark nights. And
Conversed quietly.
" So Vanessa cheated on me.
That leads me to you. I'm glad

Songs of the Black Angels

You went into the coffee shop
To meet me. I knew when I
Saw you that things were
Special between us." Said Josiah.
" My sanity is a crime in this
Relationship. I can sit on the
Shore and pass the time. I could
Even burn." Said Josiah.
" Roses entwined. That's us.
We've been chosen as super
Heroes to fight crime. We're just
On a hiatus. The water is pearl and
White." Said Rachael.
" Vanessa is over. That's the whole
Thing she messed up and that's over."
Said Josiah. " But it helps to talk
About." Said Rachael. " Those
Girls tried to take pieces of you."
Said Rachael.
" Ahnia wasn't as good as you
Made her out to be.
Let's face it." Said Rachael.

Songs of the Black Angels

Flowers fall down.
" Things didn't work out
Between Ahnia and I because
She didn't want them to."
Said Josiah.
" Just focus on you writing."
Said Rachael.
" The moon shines on the roses."
Said Josiah.
" And things will work out. As
Far as your ex's go I must say
That you over rated them. They
Weren't that great. They were
Losers." Said Rachael.
" Tell me what you thought of me
When you met me." Said Rachael.
" I thought you were the most
Beautiful girl in the world." Said
Josiah. " The blue skies go on
Forever." Said Josiah." I would
Rather write than sing." Said Josiah
It started raining outside.
" How beautiful is the rain." Said
Josiah. " This Gothic world." Said
Rachael. " And it will be ok. There
Are a lot of judgments that people
Make towards musicians and singers
Maybe you should just write."
Said Rachael. " They forgot
That people are human. Singers
Go through many emotions because
Of the judgments people make
Towards them." Said Rachael.

Songs of the Black Angels

We'd wash away with the pain.
" Sometimes I go through this
Pain. I wish I was on morphine."
Said Josiah.
" But the pain doesn't stop the
Time. I was a singer for much of
My life, but I would rather write.
And that's what I'm going to do."
Said Josiah.
" People don't need the judgments."
Said Rachael. I'll get back
To the swing of things in time."
Said Josiah. " Giving up the
Singing is a hard step to take.
Josiah you'll be alright. Sometimes
You have to do what you have
To do." Said Rachael. " I want
To write," said Josiah.
" Then write, there are too many
Judgments in music. Who would
Want to." Said Rachael. " It's
Just a big part of me." Said Josiah.
" I don't really know how to move
On." Said Josiah. " You can,"
Said Rachael.
CERAMIC UNICORNS
" But you need to know how.
Listen Josiah, anyone can
Judge a person, but not everyone
Can do the right thing."
" No, I don't want to quit singing.
I think it's just a phase. Things
Will work out."

Songs of the Black Angels

BLACK ANGELS
Bury me softly in this world.
The
Last Rising
TAMA
Leopard
I thought this was a dream.
The leopards run in the sunlight.
The illusion of your fame.
" What is there to be washed away."
Said Josiah.
" Bearing this, from day to day."
Said Josiah.
" You don't have to quit. Your soul
Knows what to do. Go with the
Choices that your soul makes.
Singing comes from your soul."
Said Rachael.
MARSHALL
" The rain will fall- you
Brought a storm upon yourself.
For no reason, the storms
Will take it all away. How many
Times have we been through this."
The leopards run in the cool ice sun.
" Follow the choices of your soul
Josiah. That's the only way your
Going to know what to do."
" I'm not going to quit singing. It's
Just what I feel is going on. I've
Thought about it, but running away
Is not going to solve anything.
The same problems will be there.
I just feel too many people are
Judgmental towards singers. It

Songs of the Black Angels

Seems like someone or the other
Is judging. What's right or wrong,
What's in and what's not. I have
To concentrate on the sacred.
That which is true and sacred,
And return to my sacred place I
Have made. The music can play.
But the storms come and go and
Take all of this away."
Said Josiah
Rachael said, " Hold onto the sacred.
You'll get back into singing. It's
Just your new wife you're worried
About."
Josiah said, " My new wife?"
Rachael and Josiah began to laugh.
" How many times has addiction
Gripped singers or musicians and
Pulled them down." Said Rachael.
" We don't need any more loss.
Singers have to stay on top. Don't
Let the fame drag you down. You're
The only one who can take care
Of number one. But you have
Got friends in your corner. Friends
That will go the distance." Said
Rachael.
" It's gone Josiah. All of the
Things we had in life with our

Songs of the Black Angels

Youth are gone. We had all
Of those friends. We had all
Of our plans. It's gone."
Rachael said and started to cry.
" It's ok." Said Josiah.
Rachael said, " I know it is."
" It's just that so many of our
Friends went down the wrong
Paths and they were so young."
Said Rachael.
" To some people words don't
Mean a thing!" Said Josiah.
" They were so young." Said Josiah.
" Well, we hope that they will be
Alright but they got wrapped up
In drugs and money. Think about
What we were like before we
Became super heroes and followed
The diamond and the gem."
" Humanity has a lot to do with
The stories of the young and
Restless. Times have been hard
And our friends chose some tough
Paths in life." Rachael continued to
Weep.
Josiah said, " God will save them."
" But they need God to save them,
And that's just not a good feeling
Right now. The whole world is in
A revolution." Said Rachael.
" Josiah we know so many
People who act like their
Lives are over because they
Are addicted to drugs or
Alcohol. They need to get
Rehabilitated. God has to
Save them." Rachael said.

Songs of the Black Angels

" God will save them." Said
Josiah. " I wish they would
Turn to God for their strength
And guidance." Said Josiah.
" It's hard to watch and stand
By. But so many of our friends
Have fallen prey to drugs or alcohol.
So many lives…"
" But the rehabs don't always work
Honey." Josiah said.
" You have to remember God is good.
Just tell yourself from time to time
That God is good. He makes the
Thunder." Said Josiah.
" I feel like Gabriel is close." Said
Rachael.
" Gabriel is close to you."
Said Josiah.
" It's like lightning." Said Josiah.
" I just wish sometimes that things
Could be different." Said Rachael.
" What's that did you forget your
Lucky rabbit's foot?" Josiah said.
" Come on." Josiah said.
Josiah hugged Rachael.
" Sometimes people go off and don't
Come back. We have to be there for
Those people anyway." Said Josiah.
" Anyway." Rachael agreed.
Rachael wept. " There have been
So many in music that have
Fallen prey to drugs or alcohol.
Our hearts go out to them."
Said Josiah.
" We're super heroes. We feel
Things differently I guess maybe the
Same." Josiah said.

Songs of the Black Angels

" They are like stars ready to burn
Out Ready to fade away." Said
Josiah. " Over the years I have
Thought about singing. I didn't
Really know what to do. Sometimes
I just want the quiet." Said Josiah.
" Oh the Devil had gotten into you."
Said Rachael.
" Josiah what is it like being a concert
Musician. You have to be good."
Said Rachael. " Sometimes it is
Amazing and other times it's
Not all it's cracked up to be." Said Josiah.
" You take the good days with the bad
Days. We have a bass player that is
Into the drugs and alcohol. It's a
Shame. But if you love Jesus you
Never lose hope." Said Josiah.
" Jesus is the hope of the world.
We should always stay close to
The Son Jesus." Said Josiah.
" Jesus understands us." Said Josiah.
" God's the one that makes the thunder."
Rachael Ray said.
The mansion was dark.
" Josiah you know you don't talk
About your feelings very often.
You always talk about
The crowds I bet. But of course I
Have nothing to base that on since
I haven't known you for that long."
Rachael laughed.

Songs of the Black Angels

" The crowds are the best part of the
Music business. The worst part is
 The money." Said Josiah.
" When we became super heroes,
Our identities changed. The original
Super heroes went through a
Similar experience. But we have
To hold onto what we hold dear as
People. And we are close to a lot of
People. And not all of them are doing
Well. There is that number."
Said Josiah.
" When we're people we're just
People. We're the same as
Everybody else." Said Rachael.
" But how about those crowds.
That must be cool I don't have
Crowds as a secretary."
Said Rachael.
" You're a real catch." Said Rachael.
" I bet the girls go after you. But
I trust you." Said Rachael.
" What happens if I make you
Jealous." Said Josiah. " I don't
Know what happens." Rachael
And Josiah laughed. Rachael said.
" that means you get some."
There lovers joked.
" Let me go into my bag of tricks."
Said Josiah.
" Better be careful what you pull
Out." Said Rachael.
" Or how much of it." Said Josiah.
Rachael and Josiah laughed.

Songs of the Black Angels

" Some people say fallen angels
Are angels that fell from grace.
Others say they're just angels
It could mean they're flying. It's
The same with the Rastafarian
Belief system. It depends on the individual
How things are interpreted." Said Rachael
Ray. " There's no cut. Meaning cut off."
Said Josiah. " Good people are good
People." Said Josiah. " Whoever
Writes this crapola." Said Rachael.
" Crapola?" Josiah and Rachael
Started laughing. " You get that
Italian thing going. Said Josiah.
I'm holding red flowers in a
Tube.
" Josiah when we were at the
Wedding you had friends. They
Had gems. Your friends mean
The world to you what happened
To all of your friends, honestly."
Said Rachael Ray.
" There are wars going on and all
Of my friends are into the
Shadows of peace. Peace is not
Prestige, it's love." Said Josiah.
" But why aren't you guys together
You still can spend time with one
Another. You should. They love
You." Said Rachael.
" The world brings me down."
Said Josiah.
" What ever happened to Robyn."
Asked Rachael. " She had a baby
Boy and she lives in Brooklyn."
Said Josiah.

Songs of the Black Angels

" Well what happened to her?"
Said Rachael.
" Well my friends don't come
Around much." Said Josiah.
" I just remember the Champagne.
We were drenched." Said Rachael.
" We had those red roses." Said
Rachael. " I'm surprised they didn't
Get on the dresses." Said Josiah.
" Not typical." Said Rachael.
" To tell you the truth I don't
Know what happened to my
Friends." Said Josiah.
" It's like a star ready to burn out,
Ready to fade away."
Said Josiah.
" Over the years we have lost
Contact. People go on with
Their lives you know." Said Josiah.
" They're probably jealous you
Know why Josiah you have hope."
Said Rachael.
" People give their lives to money.
And money is a root to the bad side."
Said Rachael.
" Your friends don't come around
Because they are jealous. Face it."
Said Rachael.
" Not my real friends." Said Josiah.
" They don't keep in touch because

Songs of the Black Angels

You're a famous singer and it
Reminds them that they don't
Have the same in their lives. I
See so much envy in your friends.
But no not your real friends." Said
Rachael.
" Who would want to be
Friends with people who envy them."
Said Rachael. The wind blew outside.
" I'm tired of their Soap Operas."
Josiah said. " It always has to be drama."
" Your real friends will stand by you. I
Can't believe you almost quit singing
You're always doing crazy things. I
Wouldn't mind if you did and put
That manager out of biz. But your
Singing is a part of our lives."
Said Rachael. " I'm a singer. I
Wouldn't mind losing some of
These people in the biz." Said
Josiah. " Don't trust some of
Those friends. They are bad news.
You have friend that are into
Heroine for God's sake. You
See these people their not with
It." " They are not friends
They're people I know in the
Biz honey. People don't choose
Those people." Said Josiah. " I
Know. I really do. I just have
Seen some of your so called
Friends back stab." Said
Rachael.
" I just want to know when

Songs of the Black Angels

People are going to give you
The respect you deserve." Rachael
Said. " I remember when I was
 A child I used to run down to
The river. I used to go to the river
With Raven. And we would play
In the water for hours. Raven
Became a super hero around the
Time I did." Said Josiah.

The Mansions of Rastafari.

" Some of the greatest
Musicians have gotten into
Drugs and haven't made it out."
Said Josiah.
" But Rachael I'll tell you losing
Friends to drugs has become a
Great part of my life." Said Josiah.
" I've seen so many people get
Trapped from drugs." Said Josiah.
" I have buried too many
Over the years." Said Josiah.
" Mercedes I like that nickname
For you, I love having you around."
Said Josiah. " And I like being
Around. And I like our marriage."
Said Rachael. Real life drama.
" I think of the rainbows Josiah.
Our relationship is like the
Rainbows." Said Rachael.
" Our marriage means the world
To me." Said Josiah.
" I know it does." Said Rachael.
" There is a distinct difference

Songs of the Black Angels

Between super heroes and people.
Your friends from High School
Are all people. They're not one
Of us in those respects. They
Don't even know about
Super heroes. Josiah those
People are not part of us. We're
Super heroes we have powers.
We're passionate about life. Our
Lives are full of victory. They
Don't have the same lives. They
Don't have the same passion."
Said Rachael.
" Josiah break free from those
People they're only going to bring
You down." Said Rachael.
" Those friends you have from
High School have made history
But it's over. Walk with Christ.
Christ is a great healer. And they
Didn't want that they wanted
Their cocaine and heroin."
Said Rachael.

Peace.

" Over the years we have drifted
Apart like waves on an ocean."
Said Josiah.

Flames.

Songs of the Black Angels

" Well they're all drug addicts
And they talk smack about you
All the time. They're back
Stabbers. You should watch out
For them. What you had is what
You had, but those times are over
Now. They are bad people, and
That's the truth." Said Rachael.

Sunnyside Florist

" Dow deep you're love is."
Said Rachael. " I guess we
Won't be seeing from your
Old friends." Said Rachael.
" You should move on is
What I'm saying." Said Rachael.
" I guess at some point I have to
Face the loss. I really don't
Talk to my friends any longer.
It's time for me to move on."
Said Josiah.
" Well they're acquaintances any way
Not friends. But they have hug drug
Problems. When is it going to end."
Said Rachael with tears in her eyes.
" I don't know," Said Josiah.
" So many people try to tell me
Who my friends are, but these
People are not friends to me."
Said Josiah. " You have to
Watch it in the music industry.
People have envy." Said Rachael.
" But Josiah tell me how pretty I am.

Songs of the Black Angels

I like when you sweet talk me."
Said Rachael. " How is my sweetie
Pie, you're brown sugar." Said Josiah.
" Thanx sweet thing." Said Rachael.
" I like when you make me feel
Like I'm the luckiest girl in the
World. Say more." Said Rachael.
" I love my sweetie." Said Josiah.
" Thanx." Said Rachael.
" Josiah, I don't want things
Another way." Rachael said
With tears in her eyes. I love you."
Said Rachael.
" I love you too." Said Josiah.
" I'm tired." Said Josiah.
" I'm tired of running. I have
Spent my whole life running away
And smack in the middle I run into
A beautiful Rastafarian girl named
Rachael Ray." Said Josiah.
" I don't know Rachael but
I wonder what it's all about. Every
Action… if I just had the faith to
Make it through. The grass is
Always greener from the other
Side you know." Said Josiah.
" Planet earth rages," Said Josiah.
" Rachael I want you to promise
Me one thing." Said Josiah.
" What's that?" Said Rachael.
" That I never take you for
Granted." Said Josiah.

Songs of the Black Angels

" I will Josiah. I promise."
Said Rachael. " The evening sun
Is setting in the dark night." Said
Josiah. " Thanks for being so honest
About the way you feel." Said Rachael.
" When I first met you Rachael
I knew you were the one." Said Josiah.
" But love there is a river that comes
Between us. This is the times now to
Catch it. They are the things that
Tear us up inside. We can't go on
Running away or not addressing it.
Crime fighting and criminals get in
The way. They get in many super
Heroes' way." Said Rachael.
" That's why we fight because
They take up our time." Said
Josiah. " With you things are so
New. You're so young. I love
That about you. It's the best part."
Said Rachael. " The earth is in
Violet." Said Josiah. " Real stories
Of deception." Said Josiah.
" All my nightmares came true."
Said Rachael. " The crimson sun
Sets at night." Josiah said about

Songs of the Black Angels

The dark world. " Take this it's
A piece of me." Rachael held
An old cloth. " Just open your
Heart." Said Josiah. " Give me
Your love." Said Josiah. There
Were castles outside.
" Sometimes I wonder about
The soundtrack to this Opera."
Said Josiah.
" Could you make it credible
And you can." Said Rachael.
" How can you explain love.
It takes time Josiah." Said Rachael.
" Our love is like flowers."
Said Rachael. The world was black
Outside. " It is like heaven. The
Kingdom of heaven is close."
Said Rachael. " Nothing can get
In the way of our love." Said
Rachael. " Your love is like
Blue roses." Said Josiah.
" I'll never forget the time
You played the en-harmonics."
Said Rachael. " You're like Indigo
Child my daughter. There is a special
Place for you in my heart." Said Josiah.
" Thanx," Said Rachael.
" We're not missing anything just
Storms outside." Said Rachael.
" This has been an honorable
Experience we grow closer as
The nights go by." Said Rachael.
" Honor thy wife, honor thy self."

Songs of the Black Angels

Said Josiah. " We're loyal to
One another. Loyalty is honorable."
Said Rachael.
" Aye." Said Josiah. " Loyalty is
Like the roses and sweet honey."
Said Rachael. " Roses entwined."
Said Josiah.
48 Hours
" Love the bleeding rose." Said Rachael.
She was his partner forever.
FAITHFUL
" Loyalty is like the roses."
Said Rachael. " Entwined."
Said Josiah. " The kingdom
Of heaven is vast."
Said Rachael. " That's what
I say when I looked into
Your eyes. That's what I see.
I see my future in heaven
With you. You're so endearing."
Said Rachael. " I see us together
In heaven also." Said Josiah.
" I see blue roses all around us."
Said Josiah. " And on the outside
Of this dream I see dragons."
" Do you know what the oracle
Told me Josiah. The oracle told
Me that we were meant to be
Together. Something to do
With the stars. Isn't that promising?"

Songs of the Black Angels

" I used to just like singing. And
Then I got into my writing. There's
A whole world out there waiting."
Said Josiah. " You make me feel
Like a little school girl Josiah."
Said Rachael. " These are such
Exciting times." Said Rachael.
" We're married and who knows
Where our love is going. But it's
Like the violets that grow."
Said Rachael. " I see us in heaven."
Said Rachael. " You and I
Together forever." Two
Super Heroes." Said Rachael.
" Two Super Heroes." Said Josiah.
" Life is about innocence really.
It's about feeling the flowers
And the breeze that blows."
Rachael Said. " When the oracle
Told me that we were meant to
Be I became happy. But you, you
Have that lead singer mentality
You're thriving for a professional
Career. You are the best singer in
The world. And you get better as

Songs of the Black Angels

Time goes on. Truly a marvel."
Said Rachael. " My secretarial
Skills just don't compare." Rachael
Gigged. " You work for Christ. You
Know that. I bet you that Christ
Listens to your work. How
Innocent it all is really." " I asked
To meet a good boy, and you
Came into my life. I'm in love.
And you think I have issues with
Those other girls you dated. I
Don't worry about such things.
I have faith. I know you're the
One for me. And you know I'm
The one for you don't you."
" Of course," Josiah injected.
" Love is mad Josiah. I think that
Every time I see you rip it up
On the stage. You carry audiences.
You are so gifted. I wish I had
Half the charisma as you do."
" Life is going to become something.
The band is going to become
Something mark my words."
Said Rachael. " I can see it now,
Especially with the background
Of prayer warriors that you have.
You're going to move audiences
And people in the future are going
To be into the following that you
Boys have so richly planted."
" Your fans are amazing people. You're
Like the Grateful Dead. You should

Songs of the Black Angels

Tour. I bet that's just what you're going
To do is tour. It's just like you boys."
Said Rachael.
" Touring is always an option." Said
Josiah. " I never knew my life would
Add up to anything when I was younger.
I see the inner city youth come to our
Shows and it gives them hope where
Once there was loss. Some have lost
Faith and yet we give them a scenario
To look up to. They leave changed
Souls. And the music touches their lives."
" We're going to be on TV." Said
Josiah. " You are why didn't you tell me."
Said Rachael. I was waiting for the
Right time." " Well now is as good of
Time as ever." Said Rachael. " Don't
Forget your dreams." Said Rachael.
" I am rich in dreams and you are
Someone I dream of. My life changed
When I met you. Just a bump over the
Coffee and there you were. Looking
Like a hot secretary." " A hot secretary?"
Rachael acted nerdy. " You with your
Jeans and leather jacket on. My were
You a site to see. A real rebel. Josiah
You're a real rebel." Rachael said.
" Four years younger than me. And
A real man. I'll tell ya." Rachael said.
" I'll never forget looking up at you.
You're pretty green eyes. You were a
Real ladies' man. My secretary work
Was getting old that day, I'm glad
We bumped into each other." Said
Rachael. " So am I." Said Josiah.
" God certainly surprised me when
We met. I should have known that

Songs of the Black Angels

There was a special other waiting
Out there for me. I never really thought
That way until I met you." Josiah
Said. " You were an answer to prayer,"
Said Rachael. " Ice is my name, but
that's what I feel towards other men.
I feel as cold as ice. You have my
Heart." Said Rachael. " Jesus loves us."
Said Josiah. " Look Rasta your
A gift you just fell into my lap. I'm
So fortunate to have you in my life."
Said Rachael. " I'm so happy to have
You." Said Josiah. " Eternity has
Won my soul tonight." Said Rachael
Ray. " Those are your lyrics. I don't
Mind if I chose them myself." Said
Rachael. " There's nothing like that
Cry guitar." Said Rachael. " I can
Pick you out of any players. You
Have such a distinct sound." Said
Rachael. " Crying Buddha is
Prophetic they are so good indeed."
Said Rachael.
" When I was a kid growing up I longed
To be a singer. Before I began with
Crying Buddha I had a similar longing.
I was hungry. I used to listen to Crying
Buddha little did I know I would be
Singing for them someday." Said
Josiah. " You longed to be a singer.
And you have a future as a recording
Artist. Practice makes perfect." Said
Rachael in her sweet and innocent way.

Songs of the Black Angels

" When I used to listen to Crying
Buddha… It's like I was destined
To meet them. Destined to meet
You. You have been my destiny. We're
Going to make it." Said Josiah.
" The oracle told me things about you.
And when I saw you it was the first
Time I had seen a star. A real star
From the heavens." Rachael said.
" You're so beautiful Rachael my
Dear. Ever since I met you my life
Has been different. We were meant
For each other." Said Josiah.
" That's why we can sit and talk
And catch up on old times. We
Were meant for each other."
Said Rachael.
" So what about all those girls you
Used to date?" Said Rachael Ray.
" Well they weren't faithful to me.
Those relationships are old and
Broken. I didn't really see the girls
After we broke up." Said Josiah.
" Yeah, but just as you longed to
Be a singer I long to talk about
These things with you. Don't
Worry about me, the conversation
Is good." Said Rachael.
" Who would believe a lot of the
Things we talk about?" Said Rachael.
" Your visions for your music are
Important. Champions have visions,
Professionals have visions. Visions
Are there to show you the way. Losers
Don't have visions. Those are losers."
Said Rachael.

Songs of the Black Angels

" Did you want to get back together
With Vanessa once you broke up with
Her or was it like a done deal." Said
Rachael.
" What a mouth. It was over when we
Broke up." Said Josiah.
" So when you broke up with these
Girls you dated they didn't come
Around again? Did you see them?"
Said Rachael. " They didn't come
Around. I saw them though. I would
See them around." Said Josiah.
" They were loco. And you would
See them?" Said Rachael.
" Yeah they were loco. Like that."
Said Josiah. " Well why did Vanessa
Cheat on you she had everything.
She had your love for a time." Said Rachael.
" She had that other guy on the side. She
Didn't think she would get caught dating
Him. But she defended them to me when
I confronted her on him." Said Josiah.
" Well Ahnia was everything to you.
And you wanted to marry her when
You were a teenager. But the reason
I don't worry about you and those
Other girls is because I know you.
I know you're not going to go get
Back together with them. We're
Married." Said Rachael. " I used to
Work as a secretary. No big news
There." Said Rachael. " No. No
Big news." Said Josiah. " But
That always surprised me about

Songs of the Black Angels

Vanessa she cheated on you for no
Reason. I can't believe you guys
Said good bye." Said Rachael. " I
Can't believe we said good bye,"
Said Josiah. " But meeting you was
Like walking into my fate. It was fate
It seems." Said Josiah. " Meeting
You was meeting a star." Said Rachael
Ray. " We just bumped together and
Spilled the coffee. I was holding
The coffee and that's all it took." Said
Rachael Ray. " You were so young
When you dated those girls. Whenever
You talk about it it's like an open
Book. They made some tough choices
And you were involved with them.
Those were hard times." Said Rachael.
" Thanks for understanding," said Josiah.
" You were so young. Love was so new
To you and it was a game they played
And lost at. You didn't know they were
Going to play games. You had some hard
Times I don't worry about you or
Your past. I trust you. And I know we're
Going to be together." Said Rachael.
" It's just strange how many losers
You dated." Said Rachael. Josiah started
Laughing. " I think you summarized
It pretty well there." Said Josiah. Rachael
Laughed too. " But when you met Vanessa
Colorado was new to you. You had all of
That hope and freedom. You were free

Songs of the Black Angels

To choose your destiny." Said Rachael.
" That's what I'm talking about Josiah
Destiny. Destiny is powerful it's not a
Drug or a game." Said Rachael. " Those
Girls played games with destiny. Sisters
Shouldn't do that. Their choices were
Insane ok. I understand what you went
Through. You had hard times… It takes
Time to heal." Said Rachael. " Yes
Everything takes time," said Josiah.
" But you don't own me an explanation."
Said Rachael. " I just think there's so
Much there that explains who those girls
Were in person that gets lost in the mix.
Your mother was a psychopath, but as
For you coming out of your childhood
It was very hard coming to terms with
This, but you had to in order to move on.
But your girlfriends seem related to
Your childhood, that broken past. But
Ever since you and I gave our lives to
Jesus we became Super Heroes. Giving
Our lives to Jesus was the fuel. Ahnia
Was your first love not your only love,
You had others but those other girls
You dated were bad news. I want you
To know that I'm not like them. I'm
Unique. And my interests
Are in seeing you move on from those
Miserable people." Said Rachael.
" Thanks love." Said Josiah. " You're
Welcome." Said Rachael. " The
Significance in your mother being a
Psychopath is that you had to see it
In order to get out of the relationship.

Songs of the Black Angels

Once you got out of the relationship
You were free from those tides. But
Without knowing you were drowning
In emotions that pulled you down.
While you were working in music. Do
I pretty much have that correct? Said
Rachael. " Yes you have it correct. I
Just don't talk about it." Said Josiah.
"Why? Why don't you just say the
lady's a psychopath." Said Rachael.
" It's not that easy she was supposed
To be my mother. I became trapped
In the abuse. Losing my voice often.
That was the only way to move on,
Addressing it in therapy." Said Josiah.
" Those years when I used to lose my
Voice were hard. I couldn't even talk
My throat hurt so much." Said Josiah.
" It was under the surface." Said
Rachael. " Yes it was." Said Josiah.
" Well the girls I dated were abusive.
They were not good people." Said Josiah.
" But you loved them." Said Rachael.
" That's the whole thing." " Maybe it is
Because I still lose my voice." Josiah said.
" Yes you do but you can't afford
Having those health factors. You have
To be able to sing." Said Rachael.
" Yes I do," Said Josiah. " I see blue
Roses all around you." Said Josiah.
" Do you know what that means seeing
Blue roses all around you
You're the one for me. The oracle said
If I see blue roses around the person it
Means she is the one for me. The dragons

Songs of the Black Angels

Are the fears." Said Josiah. " Dragons
Represent fears. Oh, I see." Said Rachael.
" Well I'm the one for you." Said Rachael.
" But I'm not like those girls. I never even
Had a boyfriend before you. I take care of
My sweetheart don't I." Said Rachael.
" Yes you do," laughed Josiah.
Baptized with fire.
Pure.
White Crystal Entertainment presents The Star Triangle
" I never thought life would be so
Beautiful. I'm so happy to be alive."
Said Josiah. " So am I. I'm happy
To be alive." Rachael returned. " It's
Been a long, weary haul to the top.
Josiah said. " Well you became the best
Singer in the world. Because you
Followed Christ." Said Rachael. " I
Never thought life would be so beautiful
As for under the setting sun." Said Josiah.
" When you lost your Dad that Spring
Was beautiful because you knew you
Were alive." Said Rachael. " I've
Followed the music ever since I
Can remember. And what I think is
Your music is about Opera. Even
Though you create Modern Rock."
Said Rachael. " But you're music
Is influenced by Trance. And that's
Why I love it. It has roots like West
African and Latin and Trance. But I
Love your lyrics the most and I can
Relate to them and others can as
Well. Lyricists are beautiful. But

Songs of the Black Angels

Trance played on instruments is
Authentic it's in vogue. It's trendy."
Said Rachael. " What is your life
Going to be being into lyrics and
Being a lyricist. You have a very
Promising future." Said Rachael.
" And you could never have guessed
What you would be walking into.
You're like a light, a star." Said Rachael.
" Feelings change, those girls walked
Out on you. Those issues were theirs,
Not yours. You probably didn't know
What was real." Said Rachael.
" I didn't know what was real." Said
Josiah. " But how could you they
Didn't deal with their own issues.
That's what I'm saying Josiah." Said
Rachael. " Head games." Said Rachael.
" I never knew what was real." Said Josiah.
" Having their issues… forget about it
They were unfaithful. How would you
Know what was going on?" Said Rachael.
" What are the nicknames of your band
Members?" Said Rachael. " Rattlesnake,
Cat, Venom, Eagle, Glory, Star, Sky,
Cry and Perry." " You never did anything
To those girls to deserve the way they
Treated you. These are their issues."
Said Rachael. " I'm just saying
At that age…" Said Rachael. " Josiah
You have to remember you're a gentle
Person. You were undeserving of the
Way they treated you." " I never

Songs of the Black Angels

Understood my luck with females
Other than just bad. I never knew
Why they treated me the way
They did. It left me wondering
Really what exactly all the bad
Treatment was about." " The bad
Treatment is about their jealousy.
They were jealous and they lashed out.
" You don't need people like that
In your life. That's all head games
they played." Said Rachael.
" You're a gem love. That's honesty,
What I think." Said Rachael.
" You're saying they were petty
Really?" Josiah said. " Jealousy, goody
Toshooes. They had it good and didn't
Want someone else to have more and
You did and they lashed out like little
Kicks." The graveyard of books and
Self-publishing lay dusty on my
Counters. What is the point in writing
If no one reads it? Writing is pointless.
In order for writing to be
Communication someone has to read it.
My writing was going nowhere. And I'm
Sorry to say. The spells would come and
Go really. Eventually I would get on to
Other things. But beyond being a writer
Was a singer, and it was a dream
That would never die. For once I
Wanted something in life I did.
I wanted to be a great singer. As for
The dream there was little forgiveness
It was relentless I just gave up time

Songs of the Black Angels

And time again. I would sing until
My lungs bled. I would sing my
Heart out. The dream tossed me like
A ragdoll. It tasted like blood. Day
After day. What I would do to
Be the singer I dreamed of. The rain
Fell from the sky. And there was
Darkness. The light my only friend.
I know the darkness. The light doesn't
Shine, just a dream. A slow lullabye. Where the
Dream would take me I didn't know.
I held on for the ride. I guess it was
All in my head talent, dreams. I
Didn't know which way was up. I
Didn't know what to say other than
I'll try harder. The long road of
Stardom and fortune. I had unquenchable
Dreams inside. I was not secure or safe.
The dreams were relentless like the
Ocean tides. Always there facing me.
Rachael was my dream girl. What
Was there to say that my dreams
Would not come true other than
Odds. I wanted something
And it came from inside. I was
A ragdoll. The nights were long
Rachael and I talked. I never thought
I would make it as far as I did. The
Good far outweighed the bad. I was
Like an inferno. A wolf. Rachael was
The prettiest girl I had ever laid eyes
On. Love and hate collided, and I

Songs of the Black Angels

Was like a shooting star. Destined
For something.
" Vanessa made a bad move." Rachael
Said. " What? What do you mean?"
Said Josiah. " Vanessa cheated on
You. She made a bad move is what
I was saying." Said Rachael.
" Oh right." Said Josiah. " She didn't
Have to be unfaithful." Rachael said.
" When I found out that she got back
Together with her ex-boyfriend it was
Devastating." Said Josiah. " Yeah I
Would imagine it would be." Said
Rachael. " You're a visionary, Jesus
Was the Messiah. Those girls chose
Poorly. They shouldn't have dragged
You into their lives." Said Rachael.
" But I know your dream like I know
Your music. And you want to be a
Singer but you want to be a recording
Artist. It's all over your work. I can tell
Just by the things you say. And you
Haven't become a recording artist
Because quite simply time." Said Rachael.
" But I had dreams of you becoming a
Recording artist. There was a pink sun
In my dreams." Said Rachael. " But
You should go for your dreams and
Become a recording artist." Said Rachael.
" Universal Records has their eyes on
You. You would be a great recording
Artist." Said Rachael.

Songs of the Black Angels

" It's all just a matter of time.
You're the best in the biz." Said
Rachael. " The oracle told me that
I would become a recording artist
Under a half moon. And it had to
Do with the stars." Said Josiah.
" Rasta you know you would make
A good recording artist it's just a
Matter of time." Said Rachael.
" Rasta I know when I catch up
To my work things will happen.
And someday I'll be a recording artist.
" Said Josiah. " But you're just a youngin.
You're four years younger than I. I
Robbed the cradle when I married you."
Said Rachael.
   The
 China
Garden
 " Peace Rasta. You're the best singer
In the world and soon you will make
It as a recording artist and you will
Achieve more." Said Rachael.
" Although there is a revolution
Transpiring, and we're staying in."
Said Josiah.
Morphine.
If I could stop the pain I would. When
I broke up with Vanessa hope fled me.
I was in this world alone. I wished at
Times that I was on morphine. That
Something could take the pain. The
World was a grey mass of rain and
Thunder. The storms that would pass…

Songs of the Black Angels

It used to be so easy to write things off.
Just to give them to God. But things
Were complicated. I reached for love
Through my faith and found Rachael
There time after time. Praise God.
" When you were in New York City
In 2001 and you were working on
In Barren Fields of Wait you were
Working out your music. I have followed
The music for years now Rasta. 2001
Was a difficult time for you, you
Were with Kerry back then. She did
What the other girls did and that was
To be unfaithful which I'm saying is
Off the chart because they were
Sisters (Rasta). " Those girls were
Just not right." Said Rachael. " They
Weren't good sisters." Said Rachael.
Life
" So you walked the streets because
You realized your dreams. But no one
Believed in you as a musician and you
Wound up being the best singer in
The world." Said Rachael.
Guess
" To be the best you have to challenge
The best. You're going to be a
Great recording artist and this book
Of fantasy will sometime make sense."
Said Rachael. Through the emeralds and
Rubies. " I went under the name
Diamond in 2001 and on in those years.
We played for churches." Said Josiah.

Songs of the Black Angels

" Governments were liberated." Said
Josiah. " Endless joy and pain." Said
Josiah. " What a glory." Said
Josiah. " Just talking." Said Rachael.
" With a very famous person. It's like a black
Sabbath outside." Said Rachael. " Where
The hell have you been?" Said Rachael.
" I'm telling you I follow the music
I know you." Said Rachael.
" You liberated governments." Said
Rachael.
Mill Pond Towers
Furniture
" Blue roses are around you and dragons."
Said Josiah. " That means it was meant to
Be. The oracle said so." Said Rachael.
" The dragons are fears." Said Rachael.
" What the world needs is love." Said
Josiah. " There will come a time
When Crying Buddha will play again.
We are prayer warriors." Said Josiah.
" The Bible says to lift one another up
In prayer." Said Josiah. " We are
Warriors." Said Josiah. " Where
Would you be today if you married
Vanessa?" Said Rachael. " You would
Probably be living in Chicago. Maybe
You would be in a band." Said Rachael.
" Vanessa wasn't your destiny I was
Your destiny. They played around with
Fate when they played around." Said
Rachael. " We were together the night
Of the Enchanted Island and the oracle
Told me these things meant something."
Said Rachael. " All of these things."

Songs of the Black Angels

Said Rachael. " In the revolution things
Are changing, more of what was meant
To be is coming true. And less of
What doesn't supposed to happen."
Said Rachael. " Vanessa wasn't
Supposed to cheat on you. But it
Happened. The long war of freedom.
People break other's hearts. But
We're Rastas we are our own tribe.
You supposed to be kind to others."
Said Rachael. " That's something all
Religions can agree on." Said Rachael.
" We should be kind to one another."
Said Rachael. " These days are like
Broken glass. Yet there are angels
Around us." Said Josiah.
" Everything is falling through
My hands." Said Josiah. " We are on
The side of the light." Said Josiah.
" But Ahnia never gave you a reason
For breaking up. She was all you had.
Vanessa cheated on you and lied about
It. She was all you had." Said Rachael.
" People shouldn't play with fate like
That. Because beautiful things are
Supposed to be." Said Rachael.
" Think about the record companies
How they decide people's futures
You shouldn't play with fate. No one
Needs people like that." " I put
Vanessa on a pedestal and she came
Crashing down. It seemed like
We would be together, I didn't
Know she was a player." Said Josiah.

Songs of the Black Angels

" You dated players." Said Rachael.
" I'm glad I didn't have to do that scene."
Said Rachael. " Love is what's important.
We should act out of love." Said
Rachael. " I remember the times
You used to cry to tears of pain." Said
Rachael. " I used to work at a tavern.
Gays used to come in and order whiskey."
I would watch the sunset at the end
Of the day. The stars at night. That's
When I believed in something, but
I have lost faith in the world around me.
I have faith in God. Before the
Revolution I would have good times. I
Knew who I was, I had my career. Now
There are battles. And battles of hope. This
World wasn't prepared for a Revolution.
Hopefully the world will heal." Said Josiah.
" It's been good versus evil. No dove of
Light. Just some on-going battle." Said
Josiah. " I wish I was alive in 1996 again.
What I would do to have those years
Back. No hidden shadows." Said Josiah.
" But we're together and the past is the
Past. We're both Super Heroes that are
 Empathetic to the world around. They're
Special powers." Said Josiah. Rachael

Songs of the Black Angels

Was everything to me she was my hope
And my joy. I loved her. " Rasta the
World is like Babylon. We should care
For the world around us. All living creatures ."
Said Josiah. " The world depends on us."
Said Josiah. " We are new creations."
Said Rachael. " I never thought I
Would be in a mansion with you Rachael.
Our white wedding was miraculous." Said
Josiah. " Our love is like stone angels."
Said Rachael. " Our love is strong." Said
Rachael. " I see angels." Said Josiah.
" I see angels too." Said Rachael.
The world was a grey mass. " Hope
Is a very powerful thing." " Some
Days all I do is talk to the white light."
Said Josiah. " I talk to the white light
Too." Said Rachael. " We were meant
To be together." Said Josiah. " With
Chains." Said Josiah.
Lion of Judah
7:47 PM
Lions of Zion

Chaos

21 Jewels

" Vanessa was a friend that broke your
Trust and who you broke up with. In
The middle of golden times and dreams."
Said Rachael. " Haile Selassie was the

Songs of the Black Angels

Leader of Ethiopia." Said Josiah.
" He was a leader." Said Rachael.
Automatic
The road back from hell
Silver Guitars
Us
Stars and Stripes
God Bless America
Obsession
Tranquility
Dare to Fly
Golden Globe
Given to Fly
Cheetah
Curve
White Wine
8 Jewels
(970) 973-2278
Firebird
Flaming Talons
Flaming Falcon
PROVE IT ALL NIGHT
0 Level
Extinguished by Light
Rock

Chaos

KORDA
HANOVER
  HILLS
Gold Cross

Songs of the Black Angels

Black Cobra
Blue Dove Cradle
Hands
Purple Doves
Red Doves
Public
Glass Doves
Fallen to Wings
Flames

     Down.
He was someone who kept to himself. A
Professional. " He was born Tafari
Makonnen. The Emperor of Ethiopia."
Said Josiah. " What led people to
Believe that he was the second
Coming of Christ?" Said Rachael.
" Led Rastas to believe." Said Josiah.
" His contributions in government."
Said Josiah.
Lyrics We hold the love
     We are a rival nation
     Nowhere to turn
     Evolution like a distant drum
     So the dream is gone
     We are marching
     We hold the love
     We are not our own

" Rasta sometimes when it gets dark
And the light is nowhere to be found

Songs of the Black Angels

You wait for life to come again. Your
Struggles have gone on for a long time
But eventually you will be liberated from
The strife and hardship. You still lose
Your voice after concerts, and though
The breeze blew in autumn newborn,
You have to stand on solid ground. And
 This is a legend." Said Rachael. " I can work
For the best record company in
The world, but it still would be
A legend. You lose your voice
Over past abuse. But you have
To pave the road to freedom.
And keep your voice." Said
Rachael. " Thank God I don't
Work for anything that exciting."
Said Rachael. " Vanessa was
A fling you're just loving."
Said Rachael. " It doesn't work
Out for insensitive people. There
Is such thing as the law. Like the
Old Testament." Said Rachael.
" I want us to make it. And you
Found the right person. We'll do
Just fine. I'm a strong lover, and
I love you. You're the only thing
In the world that I want. The only
Thing I think about and the one
Person I strive for." " You'll go
Far in life." Said Rachael.

Songs of the Black Angels

" And the same for you." Said Josiah.
Bass
" Good luck with your music." Said Rachael.

River of Deceit 2

River of Deceit

Guitar

I wanted things to be different. But they weren't. I wanted to be the best. I wanted things to be happening. What would it take to be a singer? I couldn't get out enough. Day after day went by and it got me thinking. I wanted my body to be like a clock, to never miss a practice. To have friends around. We have the power as individuals to make changes. The hardest decision I made was getting back into music. I wanted steady work something that paid the bills versus my singing career. I was practicing but quite a bit. I quit smoking. And chose to live.

I wanted to be a legend. To live with the blue unicorns.

Dead Note came out of studio music work. Slowly another band emerged. Long nights of practice and nights of rain passed.

Wish List

We were going nowhere. Dead Note was the project that launched attempts to get into the public eye and make it. Dead Note was a tour band that started out as a concept.

I always wanted a life devoted to music to make sense. I always wanted to be a singer.

Lyrics Eagles fly in our direction

Poets of a dream we left alone
Thus shines the moon
Like a pale angel
Guiding us along a path that is new
May it shine on me
May it shine on you
Something deeper within us
Greater than our souls
Black clouds, fly
The pain in the blue skies
Chariots of fire
The angels are by your side
Black diamonds, fly
The pale in the blue skies
Angels of fire
The angels are by your side
And we will get high
And we will get high

We will fly
We will fly
Black eagles fly in our direction
The Lord hears the silent lambs alone
Shines the moon
Like a pale angel sky
Guiding us along a path that is new
May it shine on me
May it shine on you

River of Deceit

Something deeper within us
Deeper than our souls
Black clouds, fly
The pain in the blue skies
Chariots of fire
The angels are by your side
Black diamonds, fly
The pale in the blue skies
Angels of fire
The angels are by your side
And we will get high
And we will get high
We will fly
We will fly

Pain in the blue skies

Lyrics Scarlet doves fly
In the oceans of your ways
Fly in the cities
Where cities never sleep
Lay down and pass
Sometime head full of lead
Did all that I could do
To get out of here
Fade out
Fade out
Fade out of the blue
You're coming through
Tire in the cities
Stay out of the truth
Lay down and pass
Some time head full of lead
Did all that I could do
To get out of here
Fade out
Fade out

It's hard to explain just how I felt thinking that my work wouldn't get out. I don't know what the long hours were for? But the publishers said that I what I wanted would never happen. I can't explain how it really felt. Or believing my work would never come out, being told it wouldn't. What did I know anyway. I'm a dreamer. And I have dreams in life. Dreams that are real to me.

River of Deceit

I wanted to tour with Dead Note. But I didn't want life on the road. I was tired of thinking about it. I considered being just a recording artist. What were the chances? Whoever said this would work? Rachael and I stayed in and it was chilling. Yet I wanted Dead Note to make it. At thirty four I sat inside and watched the rain fall. Rachael stayed with me. I could have had the best band in the world and it would still be hard. Vanessa had gone on with her life and I had gone on with mine. We stayed in the mansion on the east coast, and I thought of the Midwest. I would dream about it. Living out with the band.

Rachael was my soul mate. I wished the world wasn't so hard. Life out in the world was hard. But there was a light in my heart and faith in God that my music meant something. It had the potential to touch others' hearts. Being a tour band was powerful, it was inspiring. Making people dance.

Lyrics Fading Glory

I stood in it all
And watched the eagles fly
The scarlet dawn
I watched rise
The starlight sky
In the sunlit sky
In the sunlit sky
Scarlet eagles fly
Scarlet eagles fly
The crimson fire burned
For a long, long time
For a long, long time
I stood in it all and watched it burn
Ooh yet to learn
The sunlight on your eyes
The sunlight on your eyes
Scarlet eagles fly
Scarlet eagles fly

I stood in it all and watch it burn. The violet fire, dreams of having you. Rachael was a good thing, I had a good thing with her. Something that I often thought of. The band was working out quite superbly. There were lilacs outside my window.

Lyrics So far away from the dawn
So far away from the storm
There are blue skies

The quite storm waged on. Can we talk about blue skies? Hope
is such a powerful thing. The world was a threshing floor for dreams.
Yet, how are dreams attained, but through diligence. When I had met
Rachael I had been going through a dark time. But with Rachael life was
very different. Having someone for myself seemed to fill a void within
me. A part of me that was missing. My rise to the top was a lonely,
painful road. A path of superstitions. Hole

River of Deceit

I believed in expression, I was a singer. I believed in the good side of life. Not the bad or the wicked. Time ticked away. I wanted to live as a singer, I would not be happy with anything less. This was something to live for. Fans, albums... I saw life like a clear crystal. I saw through the fancy things for true happiness. I wanted to make people dance. I wanted to get crowds going. These were the important things to me, not money or material wealth. Instead dance and song. What makes one the best? Love. This acid jazz went on forever.

I lived for the audiences. I lived to pack stadiums. I wanted to make stadiums dance. Dead Note was the ticket to get me my heart's desire. It was a ticket on a long road of freedom.
I felt trapped in the hustle and bustle of city life. But I knew there were mountains in Colorado. And mountains in upstate New York. Mountains where I could go to be by myself. Aside from my singing success, I had my thoughts and wondered if I was good enough and if I had what it takes to stay on top. A beautiful girl sat in the room across from me. I thought about Jesus a lot. More than anything really. I thought about what Christ had done for us on the cross. I wasn't the preaching type. In fact, I really didn't talk about my religious beliefs that much. The cross... I believed in angels.

The way I saw it there was good versus evil. Superheroes versus the evil powers in the heavenly realms. I felt for the world around me, and that's something I really never got to say. Christ's compassion is with us. I didn't make a good religious type, I had too many liberal views. Most importantly there were so many lies. Lies that I had to live day in and day out. Rachael was the closest thing to me, and without her I would be lost. I had gone down those roads before, premature breakups... I didn't really talk about my life much, I was confused why or how things wound up the way they did. I had hard breakups, and I wasn't perfect. But the thoughts of Vanessa and the other girls became like ghosts that chilled my soul. How I could hold onto that which they gave me, the memories and the time we spent turned cold like winter.

Rachael and I were close, we were best friends. But sometimes love has a certain way. I was young and Rachael loved me. I was her first love, and she was the most important thing in my life. Next came a singing career. I was close to my band mates. Life didn't make sense outside of music. Music was everything to me. Girls, relationships you name it if it wasn't music it really meant little to me. Music was a way to fly. It was the way I lived as an artist. Communication is very important. Human Beings must communicate. The Gospel is what was important. In my story someone less than perfect became a super hero and found a way in the world. I found others like me. Our global outreaches as a band were positive, I was a peace keeper. I believed in peace. Rachael was my significant other.

Those times became like ghosts, the times when I used to laugh and talk with my old friends. Not everything lasts forever. But memories are memories, enough to stay golden. The times were like ghosts fading. That cold feeling. I have seen cold things. And I've lived through cold things, and dating wasn't a pleasure cruise those fantasies ended long ago. Becoming a Super Hero was Christ's perfect will and a miracle. The times faded.

I guess I really didn't think about it much, but it happened often. I would lose my voice from singing. It was a chronic problem I had and I would store my stress in my throat. It got me into writing more than anything. And I thought about Rachael continuously. So much I didn't know where to begin or where to finish. I was lost in love.

I wanted things to be different I truly did. I wanted the world to be a beautiful place all the time. I drifted farther away. I was like a ship on the ocean. Blue Roses was an album I was

River of Deceit

working on. I believed in Dead Note, I believed in a tour band. Like I said I wanted to fill stadiums. This was success to me. Love has so many ways. I used to spend my time with the Holy Spirit. Then I got ill, I spent my days doing other things, keeping my head above water. I believed I could be a great singer. I wanted to write I truly did. I believed I could make it in music.

Lyrics Crystal thorns
       On the roses
       Holy is the Lord
       You have brought me in through the water

But the competition was fierce. Dead Note was submerging so to speak.

I wanted fame. I just did. I wanted it since the time I was a child. Music is an integral part of life. It really is. But it's not a necessity let's face it. What is important in writing? Who is there to listen?

Without her I would be lost. The moon was silver. I guess it was good luck I was after. These living years were costly.

" Rachael what is important to you? In the world?" I asked.

" You Josiah, you are what's important. Everyone is different for some people it's religion for others education, but for me it's you my lover. We met in a time in life. Life has been so unreal it's like a fantasy. A fantasy that goes on and on and on. You sure are important to me." Said Rachael.

" As you are to me that's given.

" I want my music to be famous." Said Josiah.

" And who knows how the music is going to do." Said Josiah.

" There are worlds in music where you can go. This is what's important to me." Said Josiah.

" I want to reach levels and perform for people. I've wanted this for a long time." Said Josiah.

Life is a sacred thing, precious. But I was caught in an upheaval. The gloom and doom story played on in circles. I felt bound and wings clipped. Trapped in a lunatic world passing time. I would practice music, but couldn't face the pain of having to go forward with my skills. I just wasn't good enough. As far as I perceived music there was more to it. It took sacrifice.

The oracle had told me that I would meet Rachael. The oracle said I would be the best singer in the world. But I wanted more success. And it tasted like blood. I wanted to be better, but it cost. I would practice for long hours. I thought of Rachael often. I thought of her playing with children and I thought about our future. I saw people dancing in flowers. I saw stadiums of people. The essence of my desire came down to one thing and that was skill. I could sing my heart out and I had good stamina. The rain fell and I began to think again. When I was a child I would run through the mountains. I had my dream then. But having the ability to make stadiums dance was what I was still after. I had visions. It took hard work.

River of Deceit

We are all unique, and I chased after visions. The oracle had spoken. I saw people dancing in flowers and I knew what it meant, it meant the world would be a better place and that the future would unfold.

Someday I would reach those dreams. I wrote a lot and that is because I was a vocalist. I couldn't talk much, and I signed. I wrote because it was communication although I didn't know how to get the material out. The market played a large role in daily life. Like it or not I was in a situation and didn't know how to make it out. Having passion is important.

I wrote hour after hour. My voice throbbed from practice. I had to get better in order to make it. I wanted to be the best. I could do work in the studio. Thing were coming along.

The world had the potential to change. And I dreamed of the big stadiums and fans.

Joy to the world. Dance is a way life ebbs and flows. Liquid dance. I wanted to make people dance. It was a vision softly planted in my brain. From the time I was a young child I wanted to make people dance. I wanted to bring joy to people's lives. Quiet mostly when I wasn't singing I took to writing. It got me thinking.

I believe in healing I truly do. I believe in achieving dreams I had a dream to make people dance and I wanted this for my life. I wanted to be a pro musician. There was nothing I wanted more. Also, I have always believed in miracles. Making people dance would be a miracle. Prayers, that's how I would achieve this. Prayers and practice, hours of practice.

I wanted to be the best. And I wanted to be free. To play Mile High Stadium. Surely my dreams were achievable. I thought about things a lot.

Before I met Rachael I dated. Finding Vanessa was a miracle and the time we dated was filled with miracles. I realized that there was hope for my life. I always dreamed of people dancing. I wanted to get better at singing I wanted my body to be like a machine. For a time I didn't write much. The melodies weren't coming to me. I put my work down in books. Books that needed marketing to sell. They wouldn't sell on their own. But my work went down regardless. Somehow I would make it.

I would bask in the warm rays of the sun.

Captured in moments of time were my dreams. Just a baby with a dream to make people dance.

Having this dream made life different, the sun would shine differently. Things were not the same I hoped to be on a tour bus writing in my spare time. I would do anything to achieve my dreams. I wanted to tour.

Jesus and sobriety were the most important aspects to life and life and practice. Practice was a lifestyle choice. I spent hours practicing and hours writing music. I maintained hope. And I kept my sights on creating good music, and I strove to achieve my goals.

Heroine. My heart goes out every day to those who suffer from heroine. It's hard to put into words what it's like, but so many people have fallen because of heroine it's impossible not to be affected. On Christ the solid rock I stand, all other ground is sinking sand. I am determined to reach out to these people who suffer from heroine addictions, drug addiction and alcohol addiction.

River of Deceit

I have crossed paths with the greats and there has been many that have been marooned because of addiction. I strive for freedom and the burning heart of peace in the belly of a black winged dove.

I'm not a fantasy addict. Music takes hard work and daylight hours. I remember the days when I thought music did not take world and I remember the days when I thought it did. Music takes work.

Many artist have fallen prey to heroine. And when I have brushed fates with those that have I'm affected. I practice long hours during the day and day dream about heroin addicts. Being in music over the years brought me closer to heroin addicts.

The daylight barley breaks through the darkness of another bar. The daylight is a dirty gold. But putting a needle in your arm for a high invades the temple of your body. Our connectedness as a whole is invaded. The long days in Colorado were replaced by these days in New York.

And I made plans in my dreams to live in upstate New York. I had to continue the life I started in Colorado that I envisioned.

How many lead singers have fallen prey to heroine? And what matters? There was a path of gold. I was a baby that wanted to make stadiums dance.

Saint Clara

Queen's Reich

The queen held out her hand. Josiah and Rachael Young were king and queen. Kingdoms stretched across the earth. I loved her, and I couldn't let her go. The revolution had led to a new world. Good now reigned.

The queen held out her hand across the land and darkness fell. Though the stars seemed to shine brighter when Josiah Young and Rachael Young were around.

Years had gone by but the smoldering ash from the earth still rose. The world behind was ruin. Jesus carried the cross. But throughout time kingdoms had risen and fallen. A new dawn had come. Heavens had passed.